Reader comments from the *Soul Artist Journal*

"Your writing – words chosen, scenes described, emotions created – touches me like nothing else. It is a beautiful gift that leaves me vacant and overflowing at the same time. Thank you is not enough for what you give." ~ Cindy H.

"You have this gift of being able to fearlessly write absolute raw emotion. It is beautiful." ~ Susan Marie H.

"Every time I read your posts, I am taken. In. All the way. The trembling depth of your honesty and vulnerability. The courage to keep moving bare against earth, sky, along the page of your journey. The sacred masculinity is so poignant and needed in this world with the over load and over indulgence of the sacred feminine, I can only imagine someone will recognize that your work needs to be gifted to the world. Thank you for your tremendous perseverance, commitment and heart. You are a gem among men." ~ Leslie C.

"A reminder... that's what you are... a beautiful reminder. It's time to put down my 'stones' and dip my feet into the ocean. What a gift you've given yet again. Thank you!" ~ Gabrielle R.

"Always beautifully said. Thank you for sharing your lovely musings with us during the last four years! I look forward each and every week to your posting, as it *always* finds words that speak to me. I found you during your podcast time (I miss that BTW) and still play them when I need a bit of a 'return to nature' reminder. You are truly appreciated and I am ever grateful for your sharing!" ~ Susan H.

"Once again, you lift my soul to a higher place. Thank you and blessings!" ~ Shauna Z.

"Thank you for your beautiful words." ~ Barry S.

"Every week you bare your soul to the world in beautiful writing. You are my hero!" ~ Merissa B.

"I cried as I read this for it matches my world perfectly, and because tonight I feel the world's woes, and her pains as well as ours. Thank you for voicing it for me too. I'm an artist and see and draw, paint or create how I'm feeling but sometimes words escape me. I'm indebted to you. Blessings and love to you." ~ Lynne H.

"This is a beautiful bit of writing! I love your way with words. Such a gorgeous soul shines through with each one. Thank you for writing." ~ Joy P.

"I would like to say to you, dearest River... you are truly special. Thank you and thank you even more for this journey." ~ Gillian T.

"You are amazing." ~ Roger C.

"Loved, loved, LOVED this post! Thanks for putting into words... the art of food! You inspired me to go to my local city market this weekend, despite the heat predicted, where I hope to find a bit of magic and mindfulness. As always, thank you for sharing, it made my day... again." ~ SH

"Your words cause a stirring of the artistic... and a need to live more mindfully and creatively. Thank you so very much." ~ JWP

"As usual, this post resonated strongly with me and comes at the perfect time. Your writings always seem to be speaking directly to my soul, exactly what I need to hear... you so eloquently voice what is so very jumbled in my head. Your words never fail to move me. Thank you!" ~ Theresa R.

"As a late-comer to Soul Artist Journal, I have looked forward to receiving your posts. I so enjoy them, as a reminder to ponder the simple joys of life..." ~ Christine S.

"Thank you so much again for sharing your heart and reopening mine." ~ Pamela B.

"Beautiful, as always. Such a gift to read your words." ~ Randy L.

"Please... keep the words flowing so eloquently, so poetically and help more folks find their way back home to their deepest inner soul space..." ~ Mare C.

"This is a beautiful, vulnerable, perfect reminder. Thank you for writing and sharing this piece so sprawled out and open." ~ L.C.

"Oh my! It's been a while since I've been so moved by words, words that seem to speak both for and to my soul with a stirring depth and intimacy and a soothing resonance. Thank you for sharing this raw beauty, for this company on the journey." ~ Marie S.

For Meredith, who first asked for this book to come into being.

Also by L.R. Heartsong:

The Bones & Breath:
A Man's Guide to Eros, the Sacred Masculine, and the Wild Soul
[Nautilus Book Award winner]

A Life for the Senses: Return to the Soul Artist Journal

Ordinary Sacred: Farewell to the Soul Artist Journal
[Nautilus Book Award winner]

To Kneel and Kiss the Earth

Inspiration from
the Soul Artist Journal

L.R. Heartsong

Award–winning author of *The Bones & Breath:*
A Man's Guide to Eros, the Sacred Masculine, and the Wild Soul

Tournesol Press ❧ Bend, Oregon

TOURNESOL
PRESS

Tournesol Press
PO Box 1232
Bend, Oregon 97708
TournesolPress.com

Cover photo by Kristian Seedorff
Author photo by DeWeese Photography
Cover and interior design by Katie Elizabeth Boyer Clark
(www.katielizabeth.com)

Second Edition: 2024, Tournesol Press

First edition: 2018, Hearthside Press

Printed in the USA

ISBN: 979-8-218-45307-7 (paperback)

Library of Congress Control Number: 2024912279

Contents

Preface

In 2012, recently returned from years of living in Europe, in hopes of attracting a publisher for my completed book manuscript, I launched the *Soul Artist Journal.*

What began as merely a means to an end—establishing an author's platform to help promote my work—steadily shifted and drew me in. My e-column ("blog" never appealed) became a weekly discipline that changed me for the better, not simply because of what I offered to the world from my heart but the practice of writing itself.

The content, tone, and length of these posts evolved over time. And in a natural cycle of maturing, the Journal finally found its authentic voice, "celebrating a life for the senses" (though I didn't actually adopt that as a tagline until much later).

> *"How easy it is to lose touch with the tactile goodness of our days, especially when beauty seems distant, or mostly ignored and forgotten in a harried rush. Yet beauty exists everywhere. Most of us are simply not paying attention. And in both the heart and senses, too many of us are closed like a fist, rather than a hand held open in giving.*
>
> *Daily, I am seduced by moments of ordinary, heart-fluttering beauty that I love to offer forward, just as I would something from my kitchen, passed to you on a simple, handmade plate.*
>
> *Be open, my friend." (SAJ, 2016)*

In 2015, I reluctantly ventured deeper into social media to leverage my newly published book, and spent six months writing weekly articles as a featured contributor for a couple of online publications (*elephant journal* and the Good Men Project), where I learned that shorter pieces are shared more widely and help build readership. Though I prefer longer-style narratives, gradually I trimmed the length of my own posts—for a weekly column, this certainly made life easier—and, sure enough, found them flying far and wide. Yet I wrestled with whether I was being true to my vision or somehow selling out (though certainly I will never be mainstream).

The SAJ seldom focused on the material in *The Bones and Breath: A Man's Guide to Eros, the Sacred Masculine and the Wild Soul,* partly because my role in the world is larger than transpersonal men's work (valuable as I believe that to be). Truthfully, I wanted to reach a bigger audience, and there are multiple aspects to what I teach and share in life. For more than two decades I have been a bodyworker, counselor, and healer; I'm also a Paris-trained chef—one who, thanks to a healing crisis, embraces a healthier approach to food and eating than I used to. Thus, I cast the net wide and attracted both women and men as readers while reflecting on what it means to be a Soul Artist (a theme drawn from what I planned to be my follow-up book).

> *"... despite the occasional temptation to settle in comfortably and simply write about being in the kitchen, to exalt the rustic, local, seasonal fare that I love to prepare, I figure that the world doesn't need another food blogger—probably not even a French-trained, barefoot, nature-boy attuned to the subtle art of nourishing the soul." (SAJ, 2016)*

Those who read the Journal at all regularly discovered that I'm an old-fashioned, mostly quiet fellow who repeatedly encourages others to slow down and unplug from a wired existence, to take a deep breath and dilate their senses. Taste. See. Listen. Smell. *Feel.* I remind people (myself, included) to relish the pleasures of life with a heart steeped in gratitude, urging us all to savor the precious gifts of being fully human, even amid the challenges. Especially then.

> *"Life is not always art, but certainly there exists an art and soul to living—to cooking, writing, eating, walking and sitting, dancing, friendship, telling stories, making love—and it is a worthy goal to live gracefully, both in abundance and in need." (SAJ, 2016)*

Spring 2015, while visiting Paris en route to my beloved Provence, in a million-to-one chance, I met Marlena de Blasi, internationally bestselling author of *A Thousand Days in Venice* and *A Thousand Days in Tuscany*, while seated outdoors at Les Deux Magots, a famous café. An American chef who moved to Italy to marry a Venetian, and then later relocated to Tuscany followed by rustic Umbria, her lushly gilded memoirs inspired and comforted me when I too was an expat living abroad, finding solace in the kitchen or at the market. After our serendipitous meeting on the Left Bank, not only did we forge a long-distance friendship but she dove into the archives of the SAJ, and repeatedly wrote to me with accolades for my writings.

What a further delight and affirmation when Nigel Slater, Britain's foremost food writer (also a cookbook author and television personality), on Twitter praised one of my SAJ posts as "life enriching words…". I was, as the Brits say, *chuffed to bits.*

Life rolls on. I felt the gentle tug of deeper currents and unseen hands urging my vessel down a different stream. In January 2017, four and a half years (more than two hundred and twenty-five posts) after beginning my weekly venture, I closed the cover on the *Soul Artist Journal.* The time had come for a change, to turn my energies elsewhere—more precisely, to focus on the facet of work that most loudly calls to me, which is the healer's journey, and to write from the heart and soul about that. *TendingSacred* was born, a monthly dive into the longer narrative format I prefer.

Over the years, repeated requests have come from readers for some sort of compilation of the Journal—something other than the website with its archives. To that end, finally, a first collection of posts: some that I especially enjoyed or received a good share of attention, others because they simply felt right to be included in this overview and time capsule. All years of the e-column are represented, though they are not chronological or in any particular order. Just as the weekly writings were diverse and covered a wide patch of sacred ground, subscribers never knowing what topic might greet them upon opening the posts on Sunday (the usual distribution day), I have here chosen to continue that tradition. Rather than select a few categories upon which to focus (e.g. Conscious Living, Inspiration, Nature, Slow Food, The Sacred Masculine, Wild Soul, etc.) for the sake of making a more cohesive book, instead I have drawn from the spectrum of what was offered. Regretfully, due to matters of printing, rights and permissions, etcetera, the photos that accompanied the posts on the website could not be reproduced, and thus the visual allure of the SAJ feels missing here. I can only trust that the energy inhabiting the original words shines through.

Admittedly, the selections are not editorially perfect (thus, neither is this book). The weekly Journal constituted an endeavor above and beyond my normal working hours as a healer, and I simply didn't have the luxury of time for endless edits, as when laboring over a book. The Sunday morning delivery mandated that I relinquish perfectionism to a certain degree. My writing skills have improved over the years—thanks mostly to *writing*—yet I've resisted the temptation to put these collected posts under a microscope. Or a scalpel. Apart from typos or glaring style issues, I've allowed the pieces to retain their original character, full of filler words (filter words, too), passive voice, "to be" verbs, and the like. (Ah, the things we learn along the way.) The editor in me would dearly love to make the writing svelte, but I've decided to not glossy up the past too much. Keep it real.

My deepest gratitude to all the readers of the Journal, particularly those who shared the posts with others. Most especially, the dedicated subscribers and followers who ritually opened the installments every Sunday morning with their cup of coffee or tea, and the generous souls who reached out with comments and praise. You kept me going—showing up at the page, determined to offer another glimpse of beauty from the heart and soul.

Writer, healer, and cook that I am, what a gift to offer these bites and bits of inspiration for life's sometimes arduous journey. Here's hoping you'll discover a generous helping of soulful nourishment in these pages. Who can say, perhaps there will be more yet to come.

L.R. Heartsong

Introduction: *About the Journal*

{From the SAJ website}

We all need inspiration on our journey. For nearly five years, the Soul Artist Journal explored weekly the art of living a meaningful, connected existence that cultivates a sense of well-being. Though the posts were diverse, there was an underlying theme: *how do we nourish the soul?*

What does it mean to be a Soul Artist? The SAJ articles offered reflections on those little, ordinary human moments of the day: a cup of tea, a fading flower in the garden, puttering in the kitchen, a stroll through the neighborhood or along a wild riverbank. Each entry, in differing ways, extolled the importance of opening our senses and heart to the living field of intelligence we are continually bathed in. How does the moment *feel*? What is on our plate to share? How can we nurture and befriend the body as ecstatic resource for a life of vitality and well-being? What is ours to bring to this multidimensional relationship—with place, humans, earth's denizens, and planet? What is the Deep Imagination? And how do we heal and *evolve*?

The Journal traveled its own spiral and arc, varying in length and tone over the years. Yet it always sought to illuminate conscious living and embodiment, gratitude, creativity, personal authenticity and transformation, seasonal food, natural beauty, and a sensual connection with nature and earth.

In short, these writings celebrate a life for the senses... and the ordinary sacred.

Perhaps pour yourself a cup of something, and then sit somewhere comfortable and quiet. Inhale a couple of deep breaths, sweeping aside the noisy voices and demands of the day—if only for now—and take a little journey for your soul.

Welcome, traveler.

❧ ❧ ❧

Author's Note

My years of living in England changed me, both in subtle and more definite ways. Mostly for the better, I think. That said, I'm really not sure I can get through a day without teatime and proper biscuits, thank you.

In written words, a lingering UK influence is evidenced by my preference for British spellings, though I generally keep the American "z" instead of an "s" (e.g. "actualize" versus *actualise*, "civilization" rather than *civilisation*, etc.). Further, the English conventions of language and grammar (spaces around en-dashes, for instance, and single apostrophe versus quotation marks) feel and look more 'right' to me than those set forth by that American gospel, The Chicago Manual of Style. And I am rather fond of qualifiers (*some, very, rather, too, much*) which the Brits adore and employ regularly in speaking and writing, but American convention regards as superfluous and cluttered.

Regularly, I notice my inconsistency of choice(s), switching back and forth, occasionally even within the same post, as if I'm a hybrid engine. At times I have thought to comb through past writings, tidying them up, assigning a passport and nationality once and for all. I tell myself that most of my readers are American, and if I ever landed a literary agent or New York publisher, an editor would certainly force the home rules.

In the end, I have not made such changes, nor committed to either shore of the Atlantic. I'm not trying to be pretentious or affected. Even beyond writing, in matters of food, clothing, language, and general tastes, my style is an amalgam of Old World and new. And somehow this feels strangely right, reflecting who I am as a wandering, soulful nomad, gathering bits of what I like from here and there, discarding the rest.

Thus, onwards we go. We shall *savour* the *flavour* of *favourites* with *colourful neighbours* and whatnot. And I will always have a *garden* rather than a yard.

◆ ◆ ◆

A Bit of Green Magic
(March 2016)

A curious thing happened the other day. I will leave it for you to decide whether or not it was magic.

Years ago, I read a lovely little book titled *Growing Myself: A Spiritual Journey Through Gardening*, by Judith Handelsman (1996, Dutton), in which the author offered stories of her lifelong connection with plants, the special bond she shares with them, particularly her houseplants, and how they helped along her personal journey. I kept the book for an age but don't have it anymore; another casualty of repeated culling as our painted gypsy wagon rolls ever onward. Seems to me that I gave it to my dear stepmom, who is a wild gardener and hardcore plant lover.

There are two things that I most remember about Handelsman's book. The first was the author's eloquent assertion that plants have consciousness (of course they do), and that we can form a deep, communicative bond with them as part of "spiritual gardening," both inner and outer. Ever since reading her work, I have adopted the philosophy and practice of giving plants 24-hour notice before pruning, transplanting, or anything that might be traumatic – inviting them to pull their energy inwards to lessen the impact of what's coming.

The second thing that I recall about her book was how one of the stories ended. The particulars of the tale have now faded into mist, but something happened involving the plants (as I loosely recall) and afterwards, next to her bed on the bedside table, she finds a single leaf, as if placed there. There is no way for it to have arrived in that location, no logical explanation; it seems simply a "thank you" message from the plants, a living green love note that they really are alive and conscious of the communication she shares with them. And it's a little glimpse of their magic.

Personally, I believe that most *magic* is simply a higher understanding of nature and the invisible realms. At the very least, plants have consciousness – far beyond what most people would think or even guess. They have a considerable capacity for computing and forming decisions about complex variables in their environment such as light, water, sound, chemicals, vibrations, gravity, temperature and predators. They also possess highly evolved signaling systems to alert their neighbors of danger. Furthermore, they receive signals from other plants and beings, and apparently remember all of it, as demonstrated by their future choices and responses. But really, there is so much more going on.

As a self-professed Green Man, that Old World archetype of the Sacred Masculine, once upon a time, I shared roof and walls with a community of beautiful, dear plants. I loved and spoke to them all. Each time we moved house, if I couldn't bring them along (as when going abroad, or even moving between countries in Europe, or to and from Hawaii), I sadly gifted them to friends. It was like giving away my children. Slowly, reluctantly, I stopped filling the painted gypsy caravan with houseplants, and if you visit my cottage today, save for a lone purple orchid in the kitchen and pots of rosemary and French lavender outside the front door, you'd never guess that I am a plant lover with a healer's green thumb.

Jasmine grows and blooms abundantly at both at the front and rear of our little coastal house. The one in back is a considerable bush, the size of a large chariot, that has covered a good portion of the cream-colored stucco wall with a thousand curly green fingers. Particularly in the evenings, the fragrance of the blossoms drifting in through an open window is pure aromatherapy. (Note: as an aromatherapist I want to tell you that jasmine is noted for being relaxing and uplifting; in Western science, it is also antiseptic, anti-depressive, and antispasmodic. Picked at night when the blossoms are at their peak of fragrance, it takes around 8 million flowers to produce a kilo of oil, thus making it one of the more expensive essential oils.)

In terms of gardening, plants, and life, I tend to embrace a *wilder is better*, live-and-let-live approach. The jasmine has not been cut since I moved into this cottage a year ago and it has become a bit, well, unruly – blocking the garden tap/spigot, and looking to creep in through the rear studio's bathroom window.

"It's time to cut this back," my partner decreed recently, pointing to the fragrant hedge. "How about you give it 24-hour notice...?"

Now, I can only appreciate that my dear mate goes along with my somewhat unconventional attitudes and protocols, that he would say such a thing rather than simply take the garden shears to the jumbled green mass outside (though he is decidedly *not* the gardening type).

For my part, I went out to the rear of the cottage – barefoot, of course – and ran my hands through the leafy emerald riot of leaves, tendrils and flowers. Aloud, I informed the jasmine that twenty-four hours hence I would be cutting it back significantly, and it should begin drawing its energy inward to lessen the impact.

I thanked the wild green being for its flowers and healing perfume, and said I appreciated its daily reminder to simply grow. Exuberantly.

Surely spiritual gardening and tending the soul are closely related...?

The following day, during a break in the afternoon's precipitation, true to my word, I went out and trimmed the bush back to a manageable size and shape. Cool, wet earth under my bare soles, a low grey sky bearing down and the air smelling of fresh rain, *clippety click* went the long-handled shears as I cut, cut, cut. At a certain point, I decidedly heard a small voice in my head say, *no more!*

Whether it was the plant speaking or I, it was enough, really. I stopped, gently I raked my fingers through the freshly cut greenery, thanked the jasmine, and then went to work pulling wood sorrel and weeds, knowing I needed to spend at least half an hour barefooted on the earth as I continue to struggle with my electromagnetic hypersensitivity (EHS). [Read the SAJ post, "Pulling Weeds, Seeking Health," March 2016]

My "earthing" time complete and the rain beginning its staccato symphony once again, I wiped muddy bare soles on an old, brown towel at the side door and stepped indoors. In the kitchen, I placed the cobalt blue kettle on the stove for a pot of tea. Usually in the afternoon I drink green jasmine pearls, or a lovely white tea infused with jasmine flowers; both are wonderfully fragrant in a natural, non-cloying way, and I like to sip the delicate elixir from a sage green, Asian-style, porcelain cup without a handle. It is a little ritual of tranquility and grace, just perfect for a rainy afternoon.

Leaving the kitchen, thinking I would change my clothes while the water warmed in the kettle, I entered the short, meter-long hallway that leads to the bedroom and came up short. There, in the middle of the woven jute area rug, lay a sprig of green jasmine – five leaves still attached to the tip of a stem.

I stared for a long moment, then bent down to pick it up and placed the greenery in my palm. How did it get here? I'd not yet gone into the hallway or bedroom, so there is no way the leaves could have been clinging somehow to my clothes and then fallen off. The Sussex duo, our English Whippets, had not been outside with me; they were still dozing in their third nap of the afternoon, so they couldn't have brought it in, and my partner wasn't at home.

No, it was *placed* here ... by invisible hands or the wisp of a jasmine-scented prayer. A gift from the nature spirits, perhaps. Instantly I thought of Judith Handelsman's story of finding the single leaf next to her bedside, a magical acknowledgment from her beloved houseplants.

Holding the sprig in my open palm, I traced the delicate green leaves with my forefinger and grinned, a soft warm glow spreading through my heart and chest. Slowly I walked into the bedroom, crossed the brightly-hued wool rug from Spain and stood next to the large window, where I looked outside at the significantly diminished tangle of jasmine in the rain.

"Thank you," I smiled.

Gentle reader, I will only say this: in every moment, there is *far* more going on than our limited minds and perception can ever imagine. And magic exists, most definitely.

Blessed be.

◄ ◄ ◄

Inhabiting Our Vulnerability
(April 2016)

I've been living mostly *unplugged* these days and I love it, even if my Inbox for email is turning into a virtual mountain.

If you've followed this Journal for a while, you know that I have a tenuous relationship with social media; embracing it reluctantly as part of building an author's platform, and for its unparalleled merits for sharing information. Certainly there are gems and some beautiful inspiration to be found, but I find most of it pretty vacuous and a waste of time (to say nothing of being somewhat addictive). Frankly, I'd rather be sitting outdoors and enjoying the lavender flowers, the breeze whispering in the trees, and a bit of spring sunshine warming my face. Or reading a book. Writing one, even.

I am rarely on Facebook or Twitter anymore other than to broadcast the journal on Sunday mornings. The other afternoon, however, during a brief check-in for notifications, I stumbled on one of those aforementioned jewels. It was a quote by David Whyte, the Welsh born poet whose soulful work I have long admired, and I shared it immediately to my FB timeline (and then promptly signed off).

> *"The only choice we have as we mature is how we inhabit our vulnerability, how we become larger and more courageous and more compassionate through our intimacy with disappearance..."*

Yes, I thought, feeling an expansion in my own chest; that is really the heart of it. And what if, gods willing, we are actually met and supported in that bold risk of personal enlargement?

To a certain extent, such is what I attempt to do each week in this journal: inhabiting my vulnerability while also offering some measure of insight or inspiration. Or so I hope. Week after week I show up at the page, sharing some facet of a soul-centered life for the senses, and celebrating the ordinary sacred.

Here is a dance or maybe a tightrope balance: how does one travel deeper into his own vulnerability, sharing from personal experience, while not becoming too self-absorbed? When I cast the net wider, so to speak, writing along topics and stories that perhaps have a broader appeal, such as *cooking* or *nature*, it tends to mean that my posts are more widely read and shared.

I always wish to tell you something that is true and relevant. I long to write words that reach out and strum the soul with soft fingertips and evocative notes. I want to take you away from the surface world most of us inhabit, to those places where we live, laugh – weep – from an undefended, trembling heart.

Some weeks my posts are certainly better than others, and they touch more people. Sometimes they seem drawn from a deeper well, or offered in a more graciously carved cup. But really, if the Journal rings true and resonates with just one person then it is a success. As for readership counts, Facebook "Likes" and social media sharing, that's nothing but smoke and mirrors.

Recently a friend in Oregon left a message on my voicemail. When I saw the notification on my phone, I tapped it to play, switched on speaker mode, and set the device down on the table to listen (holding a mobile while it is receiving or broadcasting makes me go wobbly). My friend's sweet voice sprang forth, telling me that she had just read the latest SAJ post, and how much she appreciated my vulnerability.

"It's always like rainwater for my soul," she said, and I could hear the genuine smile in her tone.

Rainwater for my soul... could anything be more lovely than that?

Certainly I appreciated her call and dear words, the timeliness of which seemed serendipitous given my own recent musings about vulnerability. Beyond sharing my electromagnetic hypersensitivity (EHS) woes here in the Journal, the David Whyte quote set me ruminating, and I have been wading through the edits of my latest manuscript – in itself an exercise in speaking the deep truth and exposing the heart, both its songs and tears.

How do we fully inhabit our vulnerability, especially when the bulk of messages in our society tell us *not* to be undefended and exposed, particularly as men. Indeed, if we begin to pay attention, we notice that the underlying directives are almost always those of fear, telling us how to be *safe*.

Safety is largely an illusion.

From the outset of *The Bones and Breath*, a revelatory moment while crossing an

English field at twilight, the unifying thread in those pages is that *everything is relationship*. The minute we encounter a thing, we are in relationship with it. And there exists no other way to have an authentic, soulful relationship with life than to be open and relational – read, *vulnerable* – in that exchange.

We dwell in our exposed authenticity when we create and then share. Fearlessly. Knowing we must pass away, realizing that our reach will surely exceed our grasp, and that we will fall short of others' and our own expectations, what are we willing to risk in our "one wild and precious life"?

The ability to truly inhabit our vulnerability is largely determined by the relationship with our own *bodysoul*. Those who are petrified in tissues and blood, whose skin is little more than a calcified shell and the heart locked in cold armor, for them the risk of opening will be little more than a mental exercise. It is the body that knows.

I often think of my younger brother's girlfriend, an artist who teaches "brave, intuitive painting." She urges her students – some of whom have never held a paintbrush – to venture past their limiting voices and critical judgments, to use their hands and get dirty, to try something new that doesn't need to be perfect or even *good*.

This is very close to the heart of it, I think, getting intimate with vulnerability while tearing off the bandages and shackles of shame, brush (or pen) in hand. Now, bring in breath and movement to dance a bit, further opening the pulsating mystery at our core.

"Create simply to give it away, an offering the Holy, with no expectation of return," a mentor of mine used to say. Make an act of *sacred reciprocity*. Do it with outstretched arms, unfettered breath, and a great shout. Only when we go naked to the gods do they meet us, bestowing some larger measure of ourselves in return.

Friend, each day a hundred opportunities exist to play it safe, hold back, to turn away from that quiet inner voice that whispers the bare truth. Step into the circle of authenticity instead, the ring of Soul Artists.

Show me your heart, the shape and shifting hues of it, trembling and alive. I will look you in the eye and smile, take you by the shoulders and then lay my hand upon your warm, heaving chest. It is *you*, the ones who shed their armor and inhabit vulnerability as their own skin, who risk their own enlargement and disappearance, that I most want to know ... and dance with.

Come, let's shake it all loose like fools, celebrating the raw and juicy marrow in our bones, casting vulnerability so far aside that we lose it in the tall, wild grass.

❧ ❧ ❧

A Pause to Reconnect: Barefoot on the Earth
(June 2015)

S omewhere in the world it is summer.

The local high school has recently celebrated graduation, and here in the Northern Hemisphere the summer solstice draws near. Yet as I sit on the wooden steps of the deck at my little writer's cottage on the central California coast, fog swirls thickly through the trees, and the world is a shifting landscape of chilly greys and dark greens. I haven't seen the sun in a week and there's a linen scarf wrapped perpetually around my neck. Glancing at my iPhone earlier in the day, I noted that it is warmer and sunnier in London where I once resided. Summer, indeed.

In the early evening air, I pull the dark blue hoodie a bit more snugly around me, but my feet are bare on the cool bricks beneath my soles. I've been working at the computer for much of the day, held captive by the task of transferring the Soul Artist Journal to its new, dedicated website. With nearly three years of entries, it is a significant project, albeit more tedious and repetitive than difficult.

I don't do very well with computers. Like televisions and microwave ovens (neither of which I own), the electromagnetic output from them quickly makes me wobbly, a state that rather swiftly progresses to nauseous, and then I'm soon *fried* with a headache. (About a year ago, I wrote a three-part series on being electromagnetically sensitive and the negative effects of EMF's/ ELF's on the body. The posts were a bit "out there" for some folks; a couple people thanked me for writing them, a few of the more close-minded unsubscribed. All good.)

As I have shared in these posts, and also in the Appendix to *The Bones and Breath*, I long ago learned that the best remedy for electromagnetic hypersensitivity (EHS) and sickness is to be barefoot on the earth. In about twenty minutes, one feels restored and normal again – *normal* being entirely relative, I realize (most people probably wouldn't consider me "normal," nor would I wish to be).

Over the years, I've tried most of the New Age remedies for EHS, from crystals to silicon patches, with little success. That said, high-quality essential oils from woods (cedar, cypress, etc.) do seem to help. The setup that currently works best for me is an external, ergonomic keyboard and mouse connected to my MacBook, and keeping my feet on a grounded *earthing* pad. But I still get wobbly quite quickly, especially with WiFi, so I have to limit my computer time (or use a hard-wired ethernet connection, which is best). Being rather old-fashioned, I write nearly everything longhand in a notebook with my trusty fountain pen, and if I could function in the world as a writer with a manual typewriter, by the gods, I would.

As the day's already dim light fades, I'm feeling a bit fried and sitting on the steps of the deck, bundled up but with bare feet on the earth. Watching the fog trailing through the ghostly trees. Reminding myself that it is summer. In the distance, I hear the muffled voice of the sea, and the cool marine air smells just faintly of brine and resinous evergreens. Earlier, I rubbed an organic chicken inside and out with *herbes de Provence* and *fleur de sel*, and just before stepping outdoors I tucked it in the oven to roast fragrantly for a nourishing supper. Tasks of the day remain unfinished, and there are some noisy, familiar voices squabbling in my head, but as I rest on the step I push all that away and open my senses to the small fenced yard that is my existence in this moment.

The Grandmother, a venerable Monterey cypress who presides over the front of the cottage, stands just ten feet away, her great arms sweeping high, a thousand green-needled hands waving gently and stirring the mists. From where I sit, I reach out with my gaze and imagine laying hands upon her thick, roughly furrowed grey bark, as I do in actual practice each morning when I emerge from the cottage, barefoot, to greet the day in the quiet early hours.

When we extend the heart's energetic field to encompass a living being like a tree and focus on how it *feels*, there is an immediate shift in respiration, an expansion, and a subtle relaxation of musculature as heart rhythms shift (near instantly) to a more coherent, health-inducing pattern. Doing this, I feel as if I've sloughed some heavy weight from my shoulders, a sense of tranquility rippling through my being.

How important this little pause is, not merely to reboot my body's electrical system but simply to draw deeper into conscious relationship with this place where I dwell. I turn my gaze to the two camellia bushes polka-dotted with bright pink pompoms. The dark-green tangle of fragrant jasmine climbing the side of the garage. A spindly, forlorn, blight-stricken rose that just three days ago put forth a single, pale yellow offering – a miracle that seems to be the very beacon of hope, inspiration and beauty. In a less than ideal setting, not cared for properly other than the water I give it, a deep cellular intelligence has instructed: *bloom*.

Soul Artists fully understand that life is often less than perfect, that our situations are frequently suboptimal, yet still these individuals follow that inner longing to *create*. Unfurl, blossom, and shine. Like the small yellow rose and every living thing in nature, the soul's innate impulse is to be in communion with the creativity and intelligence in which we are steeped at every moment. *Everything is relationship.*

As I've so often urged, here's hoping that you will take a pause from whatever you are doing, step outdoors, and spend even just a few minutes opening your senses and heart wide. Find something of beauty to appreciate, even if that is simply a pot of pink geraniums on a neighbor's balcony or a shapely tree along the sidewalk. It is summer *somewhere* in the world, but no matter the season or landscape, blessings are abundant and everywhere. Savor them, friend.

Against all odds, may you grow and bloom where you are planted.

Conscious Loving
(April 2014)

The night air is rich with the heady scents of plumeria and *puakenikeni* outside our door, luring me sweetly to the dreamtime with intoxicating aromatherapy. How lovely to sleep in my own bed with my beloved.

I've recently returned to Hawaii after three weeks in Carmel Valley, California, my longest stretch of time away from the islands in the three years since we returned from living in Europe. I am still readjusting to the island's warmth and humidity, reorienting to the sounds of the neighborhood and a decidedly different chorus of birds. Being back, I also notice the slight heaviness and lethargy my body always feels here, so different from the mainland.

Certainly I'm glad to be home in this gracious Kailua house amongst the things that adorn and define my current place in the world. It is good to be puttering around my kitchen with its familiar spices and select *batterie de cuisine* – the carefully chosen, well-made tools, assorted objects and dishes that bring gladness to the hand and delight to the senses when using them.

Even with the easy, comfortable relating I share with my long-term mate, there's still a period of adjustment in being back together after time apart. It always takes a few days to settle into the other's rhythms, to readjust to sharing space and schedules. Realign. Harmonize. Yet it is paired with the delight in rediscovering each other again and the simple, quiet joy of savoring the other's company.

My dear beekeeping mentor on Maui, Mark, a keenly spiritual man with a generous and sensitive heart, once said, "There is nothing like being reunited with the beloved." So true.

In the long stretch of years of our loving, my beloved and I have spent some extended periods apart – for work, school, or simply exploring different stretches of the journey on our own. Some people have remarked on our ability to spend such time away from each other while remaining fully supportive of the other's path or travels, and the integrity of our shared commitment. Yet both my partner and I realize that infinite models for relationship exist, and the only correct one is that which brings true fulfillment and growth to both parties.

What is required for each to evolve into their true potential? If we are root-bound in a pot, surely we will not bear sweet fruit to feed lovingly to each other.

As a writer and artist – two labels I now comfortably claim – I'm acutely aware of my need to be in a place that nourishes my wild soul. My recurring trips to the central California coast are an aspect of that profound hunger and need, to find myself enfolded by a landscape and climate that speaks to me, where I feel inspired, at home, and fully my authentic self. It is an inestimable gift to have a partner who supports a *soul summons*, who knows that each person must follow the path that brings growth and expansion, the track that leads deeper into a dark forest to find one's soul's offering to the world.

This morning, after a late breakfast at our local coffee shop, we went together to the long (2.5 mile), sandy white crescent of Kailua beach, crowded on a Saturday with the revelry of local families and tourists alike, there to spend a little more quality time together. Reconnecting. Sharing stories and events from our recent time apart. While my mate swam in the calm, turquoise waters, I sat for a while beneath an ironwood (Australian pine, an invasive species), taking shelter from the bright sun and moist heat. Alternately, I contemplated the intricate design of the ironwood's seedpod – similar to a miniature pine cone and scattered abundantly around me – and watched a large *honu* (Hawaiian green sea turtle) floating not ten feet from shore.

Appreciating the tall, solid tree and its welcome shade, my eyes followed the noisy mynah birds and nervous pigeons competing in the sand for various scavenged tidbits, while I loosely considered what I might write in this week's entry for the Soul Artist Journal. *Relationship*, perhaps. Or trees. Both, maybe.

A few hours later, I'm gazing out the window at the grandmother mango tree, the great limbs spread wide and heavily cloaked in oblong, dark shiny green leaves. It stands at the edge of our yard and watches quietly over the tropical ravine below, a humid realm of tangled vines, feral chickens, and voracious wild pigs. Along with the statuesque, orange-flowering poinciana tree – the Prayer Tree, I call it – the old mango is a being with whom I share a relationship, saluting it each day when I step out to greet the morning, or when I take the dogs out. Barefoot in the grass, I reach toward the deeply furrowed trunk with my heart's energetic field to touch, feel, and commune with it silently, always appreciating its presence and beauty.

Looking out at the venerable mango, feeling a certain affection for trees and their quiet teachings, I find myself recalling a particular segment I wrote for my original manuscript, part of the chapter on Conscious Relationship (a chapter that will hopefully be in my follow-up to *The Bones and Breath*) in which a pair of trees wordlessly shared some wisdom with me.

ⁱ

"I trust that you'll forgive me if I make a short detour here that compares a human intimate relationship to a couple of trees I once met (though I suspect we could do far worse for a metaphor). I'll confess to an abiding love affair with trees of all sorts and have been privileged to meet some remarkable Standing Ones on my wandering journey. Let me tell you about a pair that especially stands out in the forest of my memory.

When I resided in Taos, New Mexico, I frequently visited two dear friends who dwelt in a small, adobe casita on a large ranch that encompassed a picturesque stretch of land along the Valdez River at the north end of the valley. Whenever I spent the day there or stayed happily with their dogs while my friends were away, I would walk a half-mile or so down the dirt road of the property to where it forded the river among some tall, graceful cottonwoods.

Crossing the upper pasture where Sassafras the crazy mule lived, and then snaking down the hill, the rutted track passed through an evergreen community of piñon and juniper trees where I always felt compelled to stop and acknowledge two individuals. Just slightly apart from all the others, in a wide circle of space, a pair of junipers grew side-by-side, one male and female (only the females bear the aromatic purple blue, berry-like cone pods). In a landscape of gnarly trees, both of these stood particularly straight and erect in their rough trunk, each with a similar size and a full, pleasing shape to their spread of boughs. The outermost branches between them were just loosely touching, with untold hundreds of small green fingertips entwined with the other's.

Both trees were distinct individuals and yet together they created another unit, as well—a very tangible space of sharing and relating, where little sparrows could nimbly hop from one tree to the other without ever taking wing. The expanded, overlapping circles of shade cast by the boughs offered its own mini ecosystem for all the small denizens that tend to go unnoticed from the heights of our lumbering, two-legged passing by: ants, beetles, crickets, spiders, grass shoots, seedlings, mice, snakes, and uncountable others with antennae, scales, feathers, or fur and little feet.

Perhaps it was their location, just apart from the others and close to the dirt track, but such a palpable sense of relationship emanated between these two beings that it always managed to catch my attention. Observing them, I would halt and stand for a while, pondering their long lifetime of quiet, wordless communication with each other's sphere of energy and intelligence, with earth, wind, and sky. Having stood so very long together, if a windstorm or axe felled one, would the other mourn its companion's absence? How could it not, I thought.

I began referring to these two junipers as The Lovers. On every visit to the ranch, whenever descending to the river or returning to the casita, whether crunching in boots through a white blanket of freshly fallen snow or barefoot, shirtless, and kicking up little clouds of summer dust, I stopped in front of them. I addressed the pair aloud, admiring their evergreen beauty, and even bowed to them in gratitude and respect before moving on along my way.

"Hello, lovers," I would smile.

I realize that I'm talking here about a couple of neighborly trees in a world where everything exists as relationship and an entwined love affair. The arrangement of Standing Ones in a side by side relating is hardly unique to these two longtime Taos residents; I notice it all the time when I'm out walking and roaming, often pointing out unusual pairs of trees to others I'm with.

"Look," I'll point, "lovers." (My statement has met with some rather curious reactions and puzzled responses.)

It may seem absurd to compare the richly veined complexities of human relationship with a couple of resinous juniper trees. Yet as if they were the ones speaking, these two beings never failed to remind me of Rainer Maria Rilke's eloquent and acute observation, "Love consists of this, that two solitudes protect and touch and greet each other."

Yes, exactly. Without compromise or apology, each one simply embodies his true nature while energetically—physically, even—connected to a similar being with the same essential imperative:

Grow.

❧

Soul Artists understand that awakened relationship is something more profound than sex, companionship, or happiness. In conscious loving, both partners realize that they are whole and complete unto themselves, but that their relating is the place where they overlap and create something larger than either one alone. Each individual remains a distinct entity and *circle of being*. Partners in a conscious relating comprehend that their primary responsibility and relationship remains with the Self, for only when we fully attend to our own process and growth – facing our Shadow, heeding Eros, exploring our creative nature, expanding through senses and heart, nourishing the body and soul – can we fully love and share our most authentic being with another.

Gentle reader, here's hoping that whether you are currently in an intimate relating with a human beloved or not, may you realize that the gift of conscious relationship is one of transformation and enlargement. And *love*, of course – love as a spiritual practice in celebrating the expansiveness, soulful beauty, and deep mystery of the other.

Seemingly standing alone or firmly planted closely alongside another, your life task is to root down into the rich, dark fecundity of earth and soul while reaching towards the heavens, and to offer what only you can bring to the 'other-than-human' world.

Grow, my friend.

❦ ❦ ❦

The Soulful Kitchen: A Feast for the Senses
(March 2013)

L ate afternoon. Upcountry Maui. I am peeling potatoes in the kitchen, standing barefoot on a fringed area rug that fails to sufficiently hide the ugly, old brown linoleum. As my thoughts hover behind me at the oven, noisily debating dinner, the smell of earth wafts up to arrest my attention. A hand stops mid-motion. I raise the smallish, rust-colored tuber to my nose and inhale as deeply as if it were a flower or fruit. Despite the clean, washed condition it smells distinctly of soil – a much-loved scent that makes me smile. The earthy fragrance of the potato's red skin awakens my olfactory senses and brings me crashing into the present experience. All my attention focuses upon what I am doing, riveted to the moment.

I inhale a deep breath and feel my shoulders soften, while the aroma opens my eyes and I suddenly 'see' this thing differently: a gift of Earth and a storehouse of life, cleverly disguised as a humble potato.

The French call potatoes *pommes de terre* ("apples of earth"), a description that I always found charming but also a bit odd. Certainly they are connected deeply to soil... but apples? Seems a stretch. I must be missing something.

I am working with my French peeler, a decidedly different instrument than its American cousin. It's a good tool, nicely made, and I appreciate the sturdy feel of it in my hand as I pull the notched, stainless steel blade towards me (rather than pushing it as with most swiveling American-style ones), following the contours of the potato. The thin, smooth skin of this "apple of earth" falls away in long strips, revealing the glistening, creamy interior, which gives off a sweetly chalky scent quite distinct from the earthy skin.

In all that I've gathered over the years, I have about ten favorite tools in my kitchen, each one special to me in a unique way and most of them carrying a story. This French peeler is one of them.

One Saturday while living in Paris on the Left Bank, I journeyed to the famous culinary supply store, E. Dehillerin, near Les Halles, in search of a few good tools to supplement my growing *batterie de cuisine*. Along with a fish turner and a whisk with an artistically painted grip, one of my purchases that day was the French peeler with a nice wood handle (to replace the functional but aesthetically numb, blue plastic-handled one that students receive in their knife kit at Le Cordon Bleu). The rosewood colored finish of the handle is now rubbed from a dozen years of being gripped in my palm, which somehow makes me love this little gadget all the more. Handmade, a bit worn, *wabi sabi*: qualities that I value and which resonate with my old fashioned, elemental soul.

My thoughts had been roaming elsewhere until the beguiling, unexpected fragrance transported me back to the kitchen. Peeling its skin, the soil-like scent of pomme de terre anchors me fully into the moment and my body. *Open and expansive senses always invite us home to the bodysoul.* Our senses are the threshold where we engage the world around us, where we are drawn into communion with 'other'. In this tactile, sensual connection with the food in my hand, there is something not dissimilar to the soul's solace in nature. Yes, one is domesticated and one is wild, but perhaps the word that most accurately captures this sentiment for both is *nourishment*.

How do we nourish body and soul? With equal care... or casual, negligent disregard?

My iPhone sits plugged into its sound system on the brown tile counter (*everything* in this funky, 1970's cottage is some shade of brown), offering forth island-style acoustic guitar and weaving pleasant melodies through the otherwise quiet house. After a long and somewhat challenging day, I'm in my quiet zone: spent of words, inwardly reflective, feeling some notes of blue sadness in my core but happy to be at work preparing a nice meal. As heart of the house, the kitchen is the place where I always come home to myself. For a cook, *l'espace cuisine* offers a refuge of solace and delight: a sanctuary for the soul.

Wrapped in a sonic shawl of soft music, my puttering or working in the kitchen is a sort of meditation. Making a meal for myself and my partner (or our currently expanded unit of mother-in-law and cousin, as well), it is here that I manage to set things right, even when the day has unfolded in a manner other than how I wished. It's akin to coming home and playing music on one's favorite instrument. Here, among a vivid assortment of fresh, beautiful ingredients that awaken my senses, I will create a simple, elegant meal to celebrate our connection to place, season, to each other... and Earth.

A good meal brings pleasure on many levels. For one kind of cook, a significant part of that delight is the assembly of the meal itself; a sensory, creative process to be savored and enjoyed right down to the weighty heft of quality pans, the ease of sharp knives, and the feel of good tools in the hand. Each thing offers its own chant of beauty among the gathering. For the other kind of cook, assembling a meal is largely work. Drudgery, even. It's something to be done, simply an obligation to feed the family or self. On almost every day of the year, you will find me happily camped among the former, basking in the sensual rapture of fresh herbs and fine ingredients. Celebrating life.

Today, atop the wide kitchen counter, my choice of late afternoon nibbles offers a definite nod to Spain. Standing in as very simple *tapas*, a dozen triangular slices of sheep's milk Manchego (aged six months but disappointingly average in taste) are fanned across a small, handmade pottery plate. Alas that all the delectable olives I bought last week have already been eaten. Next to the *queso* sits a shapely wineglass of crimson, velvety Rioja, "totally quaffable," as a woman in my wine tasting classes years ago used to say. Instructions to "add wine" in a recipe generally applies to the cook as well, I think.

A jumble of local, organic green beans I purchased yesterday at the market, still satisfyingly fresh and crisp, is piled on the countertop. Alongside the rusty skinned potatoes, the beans' emerald color looks so compelling against the dark tiles that I almost want to stop my work and attempt to paint the scene (never mind that I am not a painter, and would fail miserably). Sitting in a somewhat battered roasting tin from England, a free-range chicken rests quietly, its plump legs demurely trussed together with a bit of kitchen string. I've massaged the innards with a mélange of coarse salt, chopped parsley and minced garlic, and rubbed the skin with Spanish olive oil, sprinkling it liberally with fine sea salt and *herbes de Provence*. To accompany this Mediterranean-style chicken, roasted herbed potatoes, and green beans, I have pounded and whisked a quivering bowl of pungent, garlicky *aïoli* in a small mortar and pestle (the smaller of two I own, not ranked among my kitchen's top ten tools, though the larger, green marble one is).

To a soulful cook, every one of these ingredients offers a sensory delight in its own right. The tools and vessels, too. It's difficult to adequately describe the feeling of contentment – a delight that can border upon joy – from the simple act of, say, mindfully peeling a potato's earthy skin or chopping a fresh, rowdy bunch of herbaceous greens.

Creating a good meal is a simple, daily ritual in a hand-crafted life, just as surely as sitting down to enjoy it with gratitude, friendship, laughter and love. Ambassadors of good taste, Soul Artists take the time to nourish the *bodysoul*, feeding it with beauty and the blessed bounty of Earth.

Open your senses and celebrate.

Gentle reader, whether or not you're a cook (of either sort), here's hoping that you manage to create special ritual(s) that usher you deeply into conscious realms of bodysoul. A good meal invites us to expand through our senses, to emerge from the tired and confining stories of our life, and to celebrate something much, much larger.

Grace of the table, indeed.

⋇ ⋇ ⋇

Saving the Grandmother
(April 2016)

The men are coming on Thursday to cut the cypress."

So read the text from my landlord on Tuesday, and receiving it, a wave of angst crashed through me. Honestly, it felt traumatic to my soul. If you have followed the Journal a while, you know of the Grandmother: a venerable and shapely Monterey cypress who stands at the front of this cottage, her grey and green arms outstretched over the gate and small garden.

Close to 150 years old, its great trunk grows in an elegant twist, as do a couple of shapely limbs, visually reminding me that *all* life grows in a spiral (and that earth spins on its axis at 18.5 miles per second, hurtling on its spiral, not truly elliptical, trajectory through the galaxy at 155 miles per second). If you're a regular reader, you know that I enjoy a close relationship with this being; I greet her each morning as part of my barefoot ritual, stepping out to meet the dawn, and laying hands upon the roughly furrowed bark as I give thanks for the coming day. I have spent countless hours gazing at this dear beautiful tree in all sorts of weather and light, whether I am perched by the front windows to write, or seated at the round, mosaic-tiled bistro table on the deck.

About a year ago, when I reluctantly departed the seafront, poet's cottage in the Carmel Highlands, it was only the great cypress (and a fenced yard for my English Whippets) that made this marginal cottage seem like a worthwhile place to park for a while.

The text message from my landlord, who lives in Oregon, placed a heavy grey stone on my heart.

Treehugger that I am, "the men are coming to cut the cypress" carried nearly the same impact as "the soldiers are coming to take the children and burn the houses."

I have the ongoing challenge of living next door to a crazy woman. Of course I realize that "crazy" is a subjective judgment, and there are any number of people who, if they knew the workings of my own mind and belief system, would apply that same term to me (whereas I think I'm one of the *sane* ones, and that most so-called "normal" people are pretty oblivious to the deeper nature of reality). Whatever we might label my neighbor with her front yard filled with junk, she is decidedly bi-polar, swinging between manic and noisy engagement with her house projects – building shelves followed by taking them all apart, for example – and then disappearing inside her house for a quiet week. Bless her. Bless us all.

She is harmless, really, but for some time (years, apparently) she has been utterly fixated on the Grandmother cypress because it drops needles and pellets on her roof; which means that in her compulsive, crazy way she must get up there and clean it. Repeatedly. And then *yet* again. Shortly after I moved in, she cornered me about her "issue" with the tree, asking me to bring it up with the landlord; she has also broached the subject with my partner, and apparently harps on the landlord directly.

So it was that the cottage's owner recently agreed for the old tree to be cut and sent me a text, alerting me to the impending work. I suspect she finally tired of hearing from you-know-who.

Feeling genuinely distressed, I went out and laid my hands upon the Grandmother's rough, thick skin and began speaking aloud, sharing the message about the tree cutters impending arrival, and inviting the tree to pull its energy inward to minimize the impact to its being. Why not ... and what if it actually helped? [Read, "A Bit of Green Magic" from a couple weeks ago.]

When the cutters arrived on Wednesday, a day early, I explained that I wished the tree to be cut as minimally as possible, just enough to hopefully satisfy the neighbor, who is "off her rocker" and should not be listened to seriously. No sooner had I finished speaking with them and entered my gate, when she trotted out and, with animated gestures, began directing how she wanted it all cut back... *way* back.

In the end, I felt heard by the workers and was able to save the cypress from the severe trimming my neighbor desired, and kept their saws from amputating too many of the privacy offering limbs. She has had a substantial makeover and haircut, for certain, but I think somehow it worked out as best it could, and perhaps the tree is even a bit freer, healthier, and balanced because of it. Who can say, but Grandmother may even live longer and incur less damage in the winter storms.

When it was all over, the whine of chainsaws and thud of falling branches silenced, the resin-scented wreckage of green limbs cleared away and the men gone, I went out and laid gentle hands on the great trunk; feeling as I always do a deep affection for this old being, as well as a sense of relief that the worst had been avoided. I know it sounds overly dramatic, but I just couldn't live in town, in this meager little weather-beaten house if it wasn't sheltered by her graceful presence.

Though we continue blindly and greedily cutting them down, whether in our endless expansion of human habitat or to fuel the fires of industry, the great, mature trees offer something very important and healing, I think. At the *very* least, they bestow a sense of peace, beauty and joy, which are all vital to the soul. And while humans are getting better at reforesting the areas we clear – calling that "sustainable" – those new, young trees are not the same as the ancient wise ones, and Earth is impoverished for it.

Someday, when I finally find my place in the world to settle, it will be where I am not hemmed in by neighbors and streets on all sides, where I can simply step out my door and lay hands upon some wonderful trees, walking silently and joyfully among them... hearing their wordless song. Oh, how I will celebrate that.

For now, here in this little cottage in a tourist town by the sea, I continue to be grateful for the Grandmother who watches over us and sing her praises; a standing example of the ordinary sacred in everyday life, a being who offers beauty, grace and inspiration. And I've placed a purple flourite octahedron at her base, a shiny crystalline present for the nature spirits because... well, why not.

Blessed be, Grandmother, and long life to you.

🍂 🍂 🍂

Where the Worlds Touch: A Larger Story
(June 2016)

Like the windy night outside, my dreams have been turbulent and unsettling, a murky river swirling as it tumbles down the mountain. Nightly I am the recipient of messages I don't fully comprehend. Several times I wake in the dark hours, turning a dream over as I bathe in its images and lingering affect, unable to return to sleep. I hear the rats outside the bedroom window, crossing back and forth with scaly feet and tails along the wide, low sill, and then surrender back to the inescapable gravity of the Dreamtime.

Waking again, though it is still dark, I know that morning draws near, its approach accompanied by the soft cadence of raindrops on the bathroom skylight. The night's dreaming adventures have left me tired rather than rested, but it is somehow imperative to rise and greet the dawn, barefoot, even in the rain. And as so often happens, I hear a line from a Rumi poem admonishing me, *Don't go back to sleep.*

Pushing back the warm duvet, I rise and pull on hemp yoga pants and a t-shirt in the darkness. In the living room, I make my way past the two sleeping English Whippets on the couch who each follow my movements with a cocked ear but don't open their dark eyes. They know the morning routine of mine and that they're not invited. In their mind, it's not worth getting up for anyway, because their bed is more comfortable than being outside in the chilled air, especially in the rain before sunrise.

A pale ribbon of luminous grey drapes across the eastern sky. I switch off the porch light, plunging the front garden into welcome shadows, then step out and cross the glistening deck, feeling the wet cool of it under bare soles. Descending the steps and crossing the even cooler bricks, I lay hands upon the furrowed bark of the Grandmother Monterey cypress, sheltered from the rain by her broad arms that span the width of the small cottage.

Quietly I offer thanks to the morning sky, moving through my ritual of gratitude and acknowledgment. The air is heavy and damp, a faint taste of the sea, almost like a lover's salty kiss. Nostrils catch a lingering note of wood smoke from someone's chimney, ears welcome the low chant of the ocean in the near distance. All of it familiar and good, the ordinary sacred.

Holy, holy, a thousand blessings...

Back inside the darkened house, drying my wet feet and slipping them into the comforting warmth of wool socks, in the kitchen I place the cobalt blue teakettle on a hissing flame just as the old furnace rumbles noisily to life, crushing the stillness. I'm well accustomed to its mechanical, forced air voice but it still causes me to grumble each time it coughs to life and breaks the blissful silence.

I light a tall pillar candle on the hearth, and then place a tea light candle in a purple glass holder on the table by the front windows, saving the last two inches of the beeswax tapers to illuminate our dinner this evening, as I've no plans to leave the house today other than to walk the Sussex Duo. It is a *no-drive day*; good for the earth, good for the soul. I will remain quietly at home, working. That it is a rainy morning seems a perfect invitation to settle deeply into the editing work I have been chipping away at these past weeks.

Beyond the windows, the sky lightens and I observe the tops of the dark cypresses to the west sway in the coastal wind and rain. Dancing. Cup of tea beside me, my fountain pen scratches softly with a familiar voice as it trails across the pages of a notebook in a circle of light cast by candle glow. When the heater stops rumbling and vibrating the cottage, as my body breathes a sigh of relief in the quietude, I once again hear only the elemental voices of wind and rain, staccato notes on the skylight in the kitchen, punctuated with falling drops from the weathered eaves outside.

Who was I before I awoke to this blustery morning? Who was I in that other realm we inhabit for nearly a third of our lives...? Even now I am reaching back to it, curious images and tangled emotions draped in mist but already disappearing. Here at the threshold between worlds, at the edge of a continent where earth meets sea and sky, at dawn when night and day briefly touch, I still have one foot in the dream world.

In the night's final dream just before I woke, I am telling a woman in Hawaii, where I am buying a casual pullover, that I reside here just part of the year, that I live in two places. She asks if I am unwell, to which I reply that I am fine, but that it is difficult to travel back and forth, and to be fully at home in neither place. Then I turn to see that there are literally hundreds of seals, all male, passing through the transparent green waves just a few feet away...

Such is the feeling/affect still wrapped around me this morning as I ease into the day world and the light returns: that it is challenging to live in two different realms. Outside, things are returning to their familiar shapes and colors once more, resuming their day world guises. Textures are different now, so too the sense of depth, and in each moment the sense of solidity becomes more entrenched and defined, even the grey watercolor of a rainy dawn.

What is the world we live in? To which realm do we truly belong?

Moving through my waking hours, I often feel that I inhabit two worlds: a modern, technological one of emails and computers that feels strangely artificial, surface and hollow; and an older, slower life that is a sensual connection with earth, body, natural elements, food, and place – a quietly old fashioned, embodied existence that still exists and nourishes, mostly because I *choose* to make it so. Turn off the computer and phone, step outside barefoot, senses cast wide. Go for a wander in a semi-wild place and putter in the garden, pulling weeds. Take time to create something fresh, nourishing and beautiful in the kitchen. Dance. Read an inspiring book.

Yet there is even *another* world beyond those differing spheres of the day realm, one that glimmers at the edges of our peripheral vision. It slides in sideways into our consciousness when the door is left ajar, as with walking in nature, working in the garden, or deep in a creative project. A realm of invisibles, archetypes, spirits and elementals – a reality that has not entirely disappeared. *That* world, elusive and ephemeral as it is, I belong to also, one that is no less real simply because others do not fully sense it.

As a threshold dweller and "edgewalker," most of the time it seems I have a foot in two realms; one in the *logos*, one in the *mythos*, so to speak. How long it has taken me to become welcoming of that split, to understand fully that it forms the essential nature of who I am – and that it is one of the hallmarks of a wild soul and Soul Artist, the ones who are dreaming the Larger Story awake.

The rain, I hope it continues all day, serenading my soul and inviting quiet introspection.

Musing on where the worlds touch and to which realms we belong, it seems to me that the place where they overlap is always in the heart.

Do you *really* belong to and believe the stories that society tells us? Or might there be a new, more joyful and meaningful story emerging somewhere within you to share with the future? I wonder, gentle reader, who were you this morning before you awoke to the dayworld? And might that *you* be equally or even more real than the one reading this now? What is your soul telling you through dreams?

The Larger Story is calling. Are you listening?

❧ ❧ ❧

The Heart of Words: On Becoming a Writer
(February 2013)

I've been out walking the dogs to clear my head, stretch my legs, revitalize my core energy, and find a bit of inspiration. After two days of storms on Maui, it's a sunny day on the upcountry slopes of Haleakalā. The wind still rockets about the mountainside with unrestrained glee but the clouds and rain have dispersed. Finally.

Wearing my battered walking hat, I've got a dog lead in each hand, and two English Whippets are walking me briskly down the steep road and back up. Trees are talking and groaning, clacking their arms as they sway in the wind. The strong gusts and eerie noises startle the boys, causing them to jump sideways and flatten their ears backwards. The mountain feels very much alive today, a realm of spirits and a very audible conversation, and I'm glad to be a part of it.

Walking always gives me perspective. Moreover, energy. And it draws me into communion with the 'more-than-human' world that exists outside the containment of manmade walls, roof and floor. It brings me home to myself... my *bodysoul*. I'm not certain exactly when it happened but, one day not too long ago, I realized that I had finally made the transition from being a man who writes to being a *writer*. And I was thinking about this as I walked today in the wind.

Considering it, I note that the transition has been a slow falling away of my other work (primarily bodywork, counseling and coaching) over the past couple of years, like a tree shedding its foliage as winter approaches. While it doesn't exactly feel like I'm heading into dormancy, or that I am suddenly a denuded, shapely form on the landscape, there has been a natural, evolutionary quality to the transformation. Yet it's still a bit of surprise to consider myself a *writer*, as if I am suddenly now covered in new, vivid green buds and pearly shoots rather than the old leaves and vines that have clothed me for so long.

I've always been a writer, really, and I've been in love with books for as long as I can remember. I savor the feel of pages and good binding, the smell of ink and paper, the visual appeal of a fine font, the heft of a hardcover in my hand. Books are sensory treasures for me. Each one is a sensual, tangible portal to a magical realm... no matter what I am reading.

Yet like so many artists, I've struggled with claiming the proper title for myself.

For years, I relegated my creative work to the role of hobby. Partly I feared my writing would never add up to much; partly I wanted to avoid "stepping up to the plate" and risking my own success or failure. A diminutive strategy. But still I kept putting pen to paper, stringing words into sentences, steadily threading sparkling beads and stars into stories and constellations.

Real writers are published, sneers the insidious and critical voice inside my head. Poisonous words. The only antidote is to keep writing. Publicly. Fearlessly. Bare your soul.

Rather than the other identities I've worn before (bodyworker, therapist, coach, chef, etc.), I've started introducing myself to others as a writer. Usually the first question people ask is either "What do you write?" or "Are you published?" Admittedly, it does help my self-esteem that I'm peddling a substantial manuscript to publishers.

"It's a book for men on the passion, power, and creativity of the soul."

I may not yet have broken through the glass wall that surrounds the publishing world, but I trust that I am very close. My determination is formidable. Focused. I've come too far and worked too hard to turn back. And I know this: when we truly follow our soul and boldly offer something of merit to the world, doors open in undreamed of ways.

Destiny looks differently inside the Mystery.

Still, I have been struggling lately in the effort to bring my book to the light of day. In the trenches of the editing process, I feel anything but creative. Sometimes, I'm so sick of words that I cannot even take refuge in a good book at end of day. Indeed, the process of polishing the manuscript has taken so long – it's been almost two years since I wrote anything totally new – that I half-jokingly refer to myself as an *editor-in-chains* rather than a *writer*. Granted, I have a high attention to detail and a desire that my creation(s) be at the highest level of quality and skill of which I am capable. So I have been working through the chapters, carefully turning each sentence over like a stone in my hands, examining its merits and flaws, considering whether a jewel might be locked within. Is this exactly the optimum word for this expressed thought? Am I totally clear here? Do I feel a sense of flow from one paragraph to the next?

I've been mired for months in words from an editor's viewpoint: eliminating passive voice, pruning prepositional phrases, reducing qualifiers and general nouns, pulling out clichés, weighing American rules of grammar and spelling versus the British ones I prefer, all the time deliberating whether or not the chapter is driven by its key message.

Gods, how dull.

Why did I ever want to be a writer, I pout. The creative act of writing – the initial upwelling and outpouring – seems only a modest percentage of the time invested, while the bulk of hours are spent editing. Re-editing. My enthusiasm for this particular project has long since waned and the editorial work feels little more than toil and drudgery. I am willing and determined, yes, but inspiration has slipped away behind the clouds.

Last night, however, in the warm embrace of a powerful book on soulful writing, I realized that I needed to make a shift in my own perspective. From the inception of this writing project (my manuscript), I have wanted to craft a thing of beauty and meaning to offer forward. And for the most part, anchored in my expansive breath and solid bones, I have allowed the work to arise from some deep place and emerge through me.

I need to get back to that. Rather than working in an editor's stance and performing surgery with the cold scalpel of grammar, I need to return to the way of the artist: *feeling*. I dearly wish to write a book that makes readers feel. I want to open their senses. The soulful essence of the thing must come first, technique second. Indeed, if the work does not speak to the deep self, then it is mostly useless.

On some level, every reader is searching for meaning. They want to feel something. If I am reaching out to help you discover your deepest calling – the reason you are alive – I can only truly do that from my own sense of personal calling. Thus, my task in this final editing process is to hone the resonance of the words. Imbue them with meaning. Soak them in the warm, sweet blood of the still-beating heart. I will stir the imaginal, invoke the mythic, and guide you into hidden rooms where dreams dance in a smoky embrace and whisper your secret name.

As I wrote in last week's post, "I have a profound need to be fully present in my own life, to explore the contours of each passage with outstretched hands." Perhaps rather than "deliberate" living, I should use the word "heartfelt" instead.

In my personal cosmos, everything orbits around feeling deeply. Why should my work with editing the manuscript be any different? I will embody word-crafting from the heart, not the head. Rather than analyzing each sentence with the brain, I must gently stroke each line with fingertips of my soul. Does this line make me *feel?*

I also wrote in last week's post that I continue to trust in grace. As if on cue, in a moment of dark despair over the uphill journey of my writing life, an eloquently magical book finds its way into my hands to offer illumination. Inspiration. Grace, encore.

Four words now guide me in my work: *it must be felt.*

I realize that my path as a writer is inseparable from celebrating the details of my hand-crafted life. Once again I am spiraling forward and upward, feeling as I go. As a healer and artist I will bring my heightened skill at sensing and feeling into the very pages of the book. Lead with the heart, senses open wide, and note the subtle feeling of sensation within your body.

Walking the Sussex Duo up the mountain towards home as the windstorm plays around us, it seems to me that these four words apply to far more than writing; they form the directive or mantra for a soul-infused existence. Painful or joyous, bitter or sweet, quiet or raging; it must be felt. The path of authenticity, expansion, and soulful evolution is to feel deeply and be fully present to the moment and the work at hand. Such is the hallmark of a passionate life, one fully inhabited by those who hear their heart when it responds to what is presented to the senses.

Words. Breath. Passion. Love. Soul. Life.

It must be felt.

❧ ❧ ❧

A Ball of Yarn: A Meditation on Place
(June 2015)

F riday night and I'm sitting at home alone, rolling balls of hand-dyed yarn.

For just a moment, I step beyond myself and consider the scene, as if I were outside looking through the windows.

The living room with its large, wool-tufted rug is softly lit by a single bronze table lamp with an old-fashioned, Tiffany-style glass shade. On the narrow wooden table by the front windows, a pale yellow beeswax taper flickers softly, reflected in the glass against the dark night. That same table is piled with several twisted, figure-8 looking *skeins* of woolen yarn in natural hues – cream, butter, blue sky, chamisa, harvest gold, black. Some have already been rolled into softball-sized spheres, the sort of thing a cat would love to bat with its paws and chase around the floor as it rolls and unravels.

In front of the unlit fireplace and brick hearth, an upright Navajo-style loom stands with a thick sheepskin pelt placed on the floor before it. A few feet away, in the old upholstered chair beside the table with its bright candle and yarns, a man with greying but thick, unruly hair sits silently. A cup of tea within reach, he gradually unloops the skein draped over his knee and winds its freed yarn into a ball that, when finished, he will place beside the others he has completed.

Here is a scene from the early 1900's. Earlier, even. Remove the electric lamp, and the time frame blurs further. Winding yarn into balls in the quiet of a candlelit cottage is pan-cultural and nearly timeless. This could be the wild, elemental west coast of Ireland, a hut in the Peruvian Andes, or an adobe casita in the high desert of New Mexico. Wherever its actual location, it seems a long way even from the neighbors along the street, those brightly lit houses with the ghostly blue glare of television illuminating their windows.

Somewhere in space and time, here I am. Unraveling a skein and winding it into a ball is a gently repetitive process, one that easily becomes a meditation, hands traveling repeatedly in a circular motion, slowly building the wooly sphere with each pass round its circumference. Most folks would probably be doing this while parked in front of the television, distracted and entranced, but I don't own a TV. And I am utterly content in my quiet, unhurried ritual.

Suddenly I chuckle out loud, causing my two English Whippets sleeping on the sofa to look up.

"This is so damn *manly*, sitting at home alone on a Friday night, winding balls of yarn and drinking tea. Just call me Grandma."

Artists tend to be unconventional people. Certainly, some of us are more peculiar than others. The cultivated quietude of my life suits me, and while it might appeal briefly to the harried and oh-so-busy, after a day or two, most people would run screaming back to their noisy distractions.

As the soulful poet Rainer Maria Rilke wrote in *Letters to a Young Poet*, "What is needed is, in the end, simply this: solitude, great inner solitude. Going into yourself and meeting no one for hours on end—that is what you must be able to attain."

Amen, Rilke.

I've only recently begun weaving. As a writer who spends long hours stringing words together, rearranging and polishing them like colored beads on a necklace, I often yearn for something less mental. Something tactile and sensory. Tangible. That which I can step back from and actually *see* that I've created something more real than a paragraph.

I have long adored handmade ceramics and textiles, and one day the rustic simplicity of a Navajo loom reached out to strum something in my old-fashioned soul. In the craft/hobby/art field, weavers are predominantly women, so I'm upholding the minority. I've long ago tossed aside those stale notions of what constitutes *masculine*; I'm simply interested in whatever expresses and nourishes my soul in a creative, authentic way.

In our modern world, most of us *do* but few of us *make*. Our paper economy has turned us into consumers rather than producers, and the once valued practice of having a craft (as in craftsman or true artisan) has largely been abandoned. It seems mainly just the artists who have hung onto the idea of *craft*, keenly aware of its importance to the soul – which is inherently creative – and that it offers a deep sense of value and identity.

Certainly as an author, my craft is writing rather than weaving. Yet working with the Navajo loom is not only a timeless metaphor for life, the *warp* and the *weft* offers a sensory meditation, a welcome respite from pushing words around on paper (or the computer screen). In yoga-speak, it's a "counterpose," flexing me into a different expression while stretching an opposing, counterbalancing group of muscles.

Weaving on a hand-loom is slow, patient work, requiring one to be present in what he or she is doing. I love it.

Weave in beauty, say the Navajo.

There is also something in weaving that I savor as a communion with place. The yarn I use comes from a sheep ranch near Taos, New Mexico, that raises the heirloom Navajo-churro sheep whose wool is traditionally used in this sort of textile weaving. It's purchased from a small shop in Arroyo Seco nearby, where they know the rancher and hand-dye the yarn themselves.

Patiently laying in the weft threads of natural colors and beating them down with a polished, wooden Navajo weaving fork held continuously in my hand, somehow connects me not only to craft, but to earth itself. I know where this yarn came from. I have twice lived in northern New Mexico, and that wild, arid landscape of fragrant sagebrush beneath a wide turquoise sky still sings in my bones like an ancient chant.

More than *craft*, more than a respite from writing – and more than a social Friday night – this yarn weaves me into the larger story in which we are all connected.

May we all live and weave in beauty.

🌿 🌿 🌿

Cookbooks and Lemons: A Taste of Morocco
(March 2016)

For a once-professional chef, I don't own a lot of *cookery* books, as my dear British friends call them.

A decade ago, I possessed a significantly larger number than I do now (books, that is, not friends, though now that I think on it, hmm...). As a cook and self-confessed bibliophile, well, it was a bit of a love affair in the larder.

In the years of roaming the globe in our painted gypsy wagon, however, as my dear mate and I have repeatedly downsized and simplified our life, moving house again and again, I am ever less keen on packing up cookbooks and bringing them along. Truthfully, I want less of *everything*. Initially, letting go of my books was like pulling teeth – I thought of them as both treasures and inspirations, even if I seldom created anything from their pages – but eventually, thinning the ranks became easier and I seldom missed what I had relinquished.

Two boxes of cookbooks and two boxes of the others (novels, non-fiction, memoirs, etcetera), that is what became and remains my somewhat ruthless rule. Even now, if a book comes into the house, one has to go out. It's my general guideline for life, really, as I am avowed to resisting clutter and accumulating more *stuff*.

I confess that there is a part of me that loves reading cookbooks, and yes, I do mean *reading* them, usually cover to cover. The best ones are enticing, personal journeys, either to a wonderful place or into someone's kitchen, as with Nigel Slater's series, *The Kitchen Diaries*. I like cookery books for new ideas, or insights into a food culture and history, and I have learned a great deal from them over the years. These days, I rarely follow their actual directions, instead regarding recipes as general guidance: "bring these three things and then drive north towards London, but be sure to stay off the A20 or you'll end up in Dover." Okay, I can get there, one way or another.

More than once, I have joked that cookbooks are sort of like soft-porn: sexy and alluring. That said, I'm decidedly *not* fond of celebrity cookbooks, the ones with superfluous glamour shots of the chef (or their families) on every other page, posed while shopping at the market, chopping vegetables in their kitchen, etcetera. No, thank you. Let's just stick with the food.

Considering the slim troop of cookery books that remain on the shelf in my house (there isn't room in my small kitchen), one notes a decidedly European flair. The titles reflect both our life abroad and a palate that, despite classical French training, leans unabashedly towards the warm, arid Mediterranean. Boldly flavored, rustic food that seduces unapologetically with olive oil, garlic, and pungent herbs. Cuisine of the sun and sea, of passionate temperaments and dark-haired beauties... *oh yes, please.*

There are several books from England, mostly by the aforementioned Nigel Slater, whose works I adore as much for his writing as for the tasteful simplicity of the fare. Naturally, there are a few that focus on dear France, including a couple of collectibles by the inimitable Richard Olney, an American expat who lived in Provence. I have kept two books that helped me navigate the tables and markets of Spain, and two opulently written works on the regional foods of Italy by my recently met friend, Marlena de Blasi. I've a half dozen others, a couple of references (wine, cheese, tea), but not much more.

It was while residing in Andalucía, within the whitewashed walls of a stone farmhouse perched on a dry hillside, tucked amid the endless groves of silvery-green olive trees, that I learned to cook 'local' from those cherished books brought from London. Specifically, it was from the pages of *Casa Moro* (Ebury Press, 2004), one of my culinary roadmaps, that I first learned to make Moroccan-style preserved lemons, along with *harissa*, and real pomegranate molasses. I have been hooked on the unmistakable flavor(s) ever since.

A jar of these savory, yellow fruits is a perennial staple in my cupboard, and when I near the bottom of the vessel, my thoughts turn towards making a new batch. A simple but lengthy process, the lemons cure in a brine of salt and lemon juice for two months (if you're doing it the traditional way, which yields far superior results).

Cooks know that winter is the time for citrus, and the other day I realized it was time to start a new batch lest I run out (again), especially given the waiting time involved. As with most things, purchased versions are poor substitutes, even the ones from Morocco (yes, I speak regrettably from experience).

At my local Whole Foods Market, the organic lemons currently cost a dollar each; you need twelve for the jar plus another dozen for juice. *Organic* is really important in this case, because it's actually the outer skin of the lemon you use, not the pulp, thus they need to be unwaxed and free of pesticides. Still, spending $24 dollars on a condiment seemed a bit steep. Then again, the investment will last me for months, whereas a small jar of commercially prepared ones from Morocco, one that contains just two meager (and inferior) lemons, is nearly $10. In that light, the golden jewels at Whole Foods look like a bargain (well, not quite), but I still couldn't bring myself to purchase them.

Last year, my friends in Carmel Valley received a windfall of organic lemons from a friend, and I went to their house to instruct and make a large batch for them. I've been wishing for just such a boon myself, or at least an acquaintance with a productive lemon tree, but so far, alas, no.

Just down the street, tucked behind a split rail fence, a lemon tree grows in front of a vacation rental cottage. The owners live elsewhere and the tidy little house is mostly unoccupied except on weekends, when various visitors come down from the city. On my daily walks with the Sussex duo, our two English Whippets, passing the heavily laden tree I began entertaining fantasies about a covert, midnight raid. Or simply knocking on the grey-green front door some weekend, explaining to the tenant *du jour* that I was a neighbor, and enquiring whether I might harvest some of the lemons that are simply going to waste.

Regardless of the ongoing temptation, and despite my rationalization that no one was gathering and using the fruit, I have refrained from loading up a bag or basket in the dark of a weeknight when the house sits empty. Mostly the rebel in me hasn't done it because, on closer inspection, I realized that they are Meyer lemons; a wonderful, mild variety I adore but whose thin skin isn't well-suited for preserving as this particular condiment.

So much for clandestine foraging. (I later made up for being lawful and overly domesticated by harvesting some tide pools; stay tuned for a post on sea vegetables and eating the wild.) In the end, I placed my cash into the hand of the only vendor at the Monterey farmers' market selling lemons, and came home with two dozen, local Eureka beauties. *Voilà!*

In the kitchen, with a clean 2-litre French jar with locking lid and rubber gasket, along with two containers of coarse Mediterranean sea salt, I went to work: cutting a cross more than halfway into each lemon, stuffing it with coarse salt, and then placing it into the jar. Piling them in, smashing them down, and layering with coarse salt. Repeat. The fresh zing of citrus invigorated my senses, and when the vessel was full (exactly a dozen lemons), I poured in salt to the rim, followed by the juice of the other dozen fruits.

My cousin Andrea, upon seeing the photo I posted on Instagram, enquired, "how do you utilize them, and for what?"

"You use the peel," I replied. "Thinly sliced/diced, add it to all sorts of things for an intriguing lemony/salty note."

There's Moroccan food, of course (*tagine* is a bi-weekly event in our house during winter months; there's one for dinner tonight, actually), but I add the lemons to risotto (think asparagus, and you have a winning run), sauces and salsas, salads, fish dishes, and grilled vegetables. Roast chicken is another good match (and throw in some plump olives while you're at it). In my fridge there is nearly always a small, lidded jar of homemade Moroccan green *charmoula*, alongside one of red charmoula and also harissa; I use them to give a bit of zest and complexity, and the lemons add an unmistakable element to each of these condiments. On their own, the distinctive flavor contributes a bit of welcome character to all sorts of dishes, I think. Indeed, Robert often says, "Oh, I can taste the Moroccan lemon... I love that!"

Gentle reader, we're definitely walking the domestic side this week rather than the wild, but like so much of what appeals to me in the kitchen – as with the heart of good cooking – making preserved lemons is a tactile ritual that nourishes the senses, body and soul. It is yet another simple celebration of the goodness of earth and nature, along with the sensual gift of being alive. Breathing in, breathing out. The ordinary sacred, right here in our hands.

Perhaps if you're feeling adventurous and are willing to wait for the final reward, strike out and try something new. Ancient, rather. Investing time in this culinary gold is an old-fashioned pursuit that yields an utterly intriguing and delicious result, and you're likely to have a bit of fun in the process. Very little is better than that, I say (barefoot foraging on a wild hillside, notwithstanding).

Bring on the lemons and coarse salt.

A Recipe: Moroccan-style Preserved Lemons

Ingredients:

12 organic lemons (not the Meyer variety)
10-12 additional lemons for juicing (roughly 1 to 2 cups juice)
1 kg coarse salt (or kosher, which yields a slightly less salty result)
2 litre/quart glass jar, sterilized

Method:

Begin by cutting a deep cross into each lemon (as if you were going to cut it in half, but stopping short of cutting all the way through). Spread the quarters open and pack/pour in as much salt as possible, and press together again. It helps to do this work over a large bowl to catch the salt, which can be used later to fill the jar. Place each cut and filled lemon into the clean jar, alternating salt and lemons, until the jar is full.

Cut and then juice the remaining dozen fruits. Press down to help extrude the juice of the ones in the jar, and then pour in the extra lemon juice so that the contents are covered completely. Add more salt if needed to raise the liquid level to the top of the jar. Close and seal, then set aside for a day.

The next day, check to see if any of the lemons have risen up to break the surface; if they have, push them back down into the liquid, and adding more lemon juice/ salt if needed to cover. Turning the jar upside down will redistribute the salt more evenly. (There is generally no need to check the jar after the first day.) With all the fruit submerged, place your cache in a cool, dark place for 2 months. Once they have finished curing, the skins should be soft all the way through.

You can add things like spices and chiles to the jar, and it certainly looks attractive, but such elements won't affect the taste of the lemons much (though chiles can contribute a bite) only the brine.

❧

To use the preserved fruit, take a lemon from the jar, discard the inner pulp, and then rinse the skin under cold water to remove excess brine and salt. Chop finely and add to your recipe, or scatter atop of a dish as a garnish.

(Note: because the lemons are salty, be mindful of the amount of salt you add to a dish before adding the peel.)

Opened, there is no need to refrigerate the jar as long as the remaining lemons are covered in liquid. Having a jar of Moroccan-style lemons sitting on your countertop adds an intriguing note to your kitchen, and also prompts you to use them and experiment.

Lemons are at their peak at 3 to 4 months but will keep for up to a year; removed from the brine, they can be kept covered with oil indefinitely. They may eventually discolor, but this is not a sign of spoilage.

Serving ideas: if a food generally goes well with lemon and salt, then preserved lemon is probably a good match and will add a unique depth of flavor. Try the minced peel with olives, green salsas, with vegetables, fish, in salads, in risotto or pasta, with couscous... the possibilities abound

❧ ❧ ❧

The Shaman of Stars

(July 2016)

I wake in the night to a pale glow of moonlight illuminating the thick linen draperies, as if they were somehow spun of the luminous pearl outside in the heavens.

Freshly emerged from the cocoon of the Dreamtime, still wrapped in silken images and the warm breath of feelings, I drink in the quietude of my bedroom and the cottage. Hovering at the threshold between worlds, I listen for the chant of the sea but hear no trace of its timeless voice. As so often happens, even sometimes during my daylight hours, I see myself in another place and time, an imagined world or parallel reality. For a moment, I am alone outdoors in some wild, high place, turned toward the sunlight in a blue sky and a fair coastal wind.

Stand here, facing the sun and rain, rooted as if a tree, I think. Embrace this moment. Whatever arrives, be it hummingbird or lightning bolt, welcome it. *All things are becoming.*

For some time now, I have been shadowed and stalked by a sense of impending change, that a big shift is unfolding – that in some invisible way that I am already *in* that new phase, even if I do not yet perceive the physical changes in my daily world of work, place, and human relationships. Can a rose detect its own growth process, even if its bud has not yet appeared?

I discern that somehow I am shifting, becoming subtly more open and expansive; less attached to old ways of thinking, grasping, and holding. Simultaneously I am more cognizant and aware of the chosen limitations and doubts that I've clung to for so long, as if each was some priceless treasure. I see that each strategy and habit has served me in its own way (protection, comfort, etcetera) yet has also outlived its usefulness.

Change hovers in the air like a scent carried by the wind. It stirs under my feet as the earth dreams us awake, and I feel and hear the quiet, wordless summons.

Surely we all know the small voice that whispers from somewhere beyond the horizon, even if we fear listening to it. Rather than feel our deep longing or the soft echo of thunder in our bones, calling and daring us to something larger, instead we turn up the music or television. How much easier and safer it is to remain numb and distracted. Just keep busy, we tell ourselves, turning back to our phone and emails, our breath shallow and tight.

Yet the larger story is always unfurling in our lives, guiding the little vessel of bodysoul on unfathomable currents that defy logic and tidy charts, even those predictable orbits of sun and moon. And each of us is continually called to become something more authentic despite the risks of that process, and regardless of the challenges and setbacks of such a hazardous but rewarding journey.

As a soul, what did you come back here to learn, do, and offer? And isn't finding the answer to that question the quest of a lifetime?

In the pale silver light of the darkened bedroom, alone in our bed, my partner away, I quietly follow the tides of my breath in and out, feeling ever more acutely that something is *happening* in my life, even if still unseen or unformed. I sense it as surely as a smooth, green stone pressed into the warmth of my open palm.

Here, now, River, root down into this place and spread your limbs – branches, wings – and heart wide to the sky, as if you are the Shaman of Stars, calling down the song of the heavens as a blessing that transforms all of life. Become the Hunter of Dreams and the Bearer of Gifts, using those winged arms to fly above any sorrows and remnants of a life too small.

The only constant is change.

All energy is movement, and movement is life. When that current stops, both literally and figuratively we die. And yet so many of us feel trapped amid the circumstances that seemingly conspire in keeping us in stasis and stagnation. What are we truly willing to let go of – accomplishments? limitations? identity? – that keeps us tethered to the safety of the riverbank, even as the river's silvery green hands knock and pull at the hull of our little boat...?

Time now to cast off and let go the rudder, despite not knowing what we will meet around the next bend. It might be whitewater rapids or a waterfall, yet it may simply be a wide open, graceful river flowing surely to the sea. We won't know until we meet it and pass through, broken open or seemingly intact.

In the milky darkness and quietude, a foot in two worlds, turning the moonstone over in my palm and looking for its inscription or guidance, like so many times before, I hear the lines of a Rumi poem translated by Coleman Barks, reminding me:

> *The breeze at dawn has secrets to tell you.*
> *Don't go back to sleep.*
> *You must ask for what you really want.*
> *Don't go back to sleep.*
> *People are going back and forth across the doorsill*
> *where the two worlds touch.*
> *The door is round and open.*
> *Don't go back to sleep.*

Friend, if we're on a conscious journey in life (or even if we are not), each in our own unique ways we are growing into something larger. *All things are becoming.* And the story is SO much bigger than the nightly news, with its circus of politics and all the heartache in the world.

Keeping your fist clenched tight – in grasping, fear, anger – means that your palm cannot receive. Choose instead to let go and open, to fall into the depths of your longing. And gratitude.

Consider that, for better or worse, the entire Universe has conspired to bring this moment about. No matter your surroundings and circumstance, your only real task is to gather in and share as much beauty as you're able to, while you endeavor to become the most authentic and undefended version of yourself possible. Everything else is too small for you.

Dawn arrives eventually. *Don't go back to sleep.*

As you grow and change, dare to tell the truth, I say, even if others don't understand your perspective. *Especially* then. And whether in the moon's glow or light of day, no matter your chosen path, may you look inside your heart and find the Shaman of Stars, singing down the heavens to guide you further along the mysterious journey.

🌿 🌿 🌿

Leaving My Shoes Along the Trail
(September 2015)

~ Part 1: Severance

I admit to a conflicted relationship with Big Sur, the vast and sparsely inhabited coastal region immediately south of Carmel, California. A land of dramatic hillsides and cliffs meeting the sea, a narrow winding highway (often closed for rockslides, or un-navigable due to thick fog), and an untamed wilderness. As the rugged, raw threshold of a continent, where earth greets sea and sky, for all of its wildness and scenic beauty, I should love it – and I *do*, but for the fact that it is simply overrun with tourists, especially in the summer.

I find myself residing on the northern edge of this deeply alluring region that whispers to my soul continuously, yet I resist its magic for months at a time because of the people, most of them loud and boisterous urban dwellers.

Everything is relative, I suppose. If you live in the tightly crowded, noisy grid of the city, arriving in Big Sur it seems uncrowded and expansive (apart from the long stream of cars and motorhomes). If, however, you dwell in a very small, quiet town at the edge of that majestic wilderness, Big Sur can feel less than inviting – at least until after Thanksgiving, when the flocks of folks finally disperse and winter storms roll in.

I've been feeling restless lately. Partly it is the soft call of autumn drawing near, a familiar wanderlust that rises in me each Fall – especially if I haven't wandered sufficiently in wild places of the earth. I've spent too much of this summer in town, holed up in my cottage beneath the great Monterey cypress tree, working and writing... avoiding Big Sur and its steady queue of traffic.

My life is constructed around soulful rituals, artisan things, and practices that nourish me daily on a deep level: greeting the dawn barefoot, movement and breath, a home that feels like a sanctuary, making beautiful fresh food, quiet evenings by candlelight. Yet my wild soul still needs to immerse itself in non-domesticated nature. Regularly. For me, it's like plunging into a pool on a hot summer day – suddenly everything is good again, all the heat, sweat, and irritation washed away.

I know from the restlessness in my core, the growing sense of grumbling and overwhelm, that what I really need is to pull the plug and disappear into a redwood canyon for awhile. (This being more practical than running off to New Mexico to wander a sage-strewn mesa at the foot of Taos Mountain.) *Disconnect to reconnect.*

Saturday is never a good choice for going into Big Sur. Because of a client in the early afternoon, I can't simply head out with zero agenda and venture deeper into the region where the crowds are thinner. Repeatedly, considering this trek, I find myself bumping into my own reluctance over going.

That's the story of my life, it seems, *bumping into my own resistance*, but I'm much better at dancing with it these days.

While it's true that it won't be solitude, even a brief escape into nature will still feed my soul. I stash a few essentials in my small Osprey daypack – water bottle, Pink Lady apple, raw almonds, my little black journal and fountain pen, a grey soft-shell jacket – and pull on Keen hiking sandals. Grabbing my battered walking hat, I head out. My mate is working in Hawaii, and I'm leaving the Sussex Duo at home; ignoring their downcast, plaintive expressions that I am going on an adventure without them. I love my English Whippets but being with them on a walk changes everything. Today is solo time, not a family outing.

ↁ

I arrive early enough that I find parking close to the trailhead, an encouraging sign, and stepping through the gate, all seems quiet and uncrowded. Already I feel a quickening in my core, a bubbling up of energy and excitement, and a little grin on my face. Oh yes, I *needed* this.

The morning shines bright and warm, a clear blue sky singing overhead, and as I walk toward the mouth of the coastal canyon, the briny scent and surging voice of the sea quickly fades. Instead I am enfolded by the vaguely sage-like scent of chaparral and late summer brush. Red leaves of poison oak are stitched amid the landscape, easier to spot this time of year than in its green stage, adding a dramatic element of color. My eye is also drawn here and there by the errant golden poppy, a few fading wildflowers, even the odd Morning Glory blossom on a creeping vine.

I've not walked here since spring and I'm struck by how parched everything is. California is struggling in its fourth year of severe drought; half the state is on fire, it seems. As I tread along the dusty trail with my senses cast wide to the late summer beauty, intent on feeling what surrounds me, what I most sense is *thirst*.

I know that just ahead there is a small stream crossing, but even before I reach the cluster of leafy trees or see the water, I smell it – a cool, faintly sweet scent in the air. It's surprising to me that the creek still flows in early September, especially when there seems to be virtually no water elsewhere in the land. Unbidden, a tender, strong gladness rises up in my heart, knowing that the wild ones – cougar, deer, bobcat, coyote, fox, badger – can find a drink here in this long, dry season.

The path crosses this shallow waterway several times in the low reaches of the canyon, then follows alongside as the rise grows steeper, finally leaving it behind and climbing the ridge above the redwoods. Approaching the second crossing, I hear the familiar sonic drone of bees, and the beekeeper in me rejoices with a smile as I scan for them.

The water here is slow and barely three-inches deep, and the air hums with thirsty bees as they alight on the sandy edge of the stream. Bees need water, too. I flash briefly back to living in southern Spain, to the rugged canyon behind our whitewashed farmhouse amid the olive groves where I often walked. High in the gorge, a stretch of the dusty path ran alongside an old *acequia*, still flowing, and there was a particular open, sandy section of the bank that was usually lined with wild honeybees. I would stop and crouch down to watch them, a hundred golden, furry bodies lined up on each side of the stream, drinking from the water's edge. Bless them.

They are in trouble, these winged alchemists of nature, fighting not only the varroa mite but also being poisoned across the globe by the neonicotinoids bred into GMO crops. Offering them a silent blessing of thanks on the stream bank, a prayer for their survival, I move on.

∾

Ascending the gradual incline, with every step I feel my body, senses, and soul becoming more expansive. I'm sloughing off troubles and dissatisfactions, the mundane work that has confined me, shedding a skin too small. I take longer strides, encouraging creaky hips to open as I consciously deepen my breath. Here, now, I am reemerging from the patterns I repeatedly slip into when I don't dance, move, or get outside enough (something more than simply walking the Whippets through the neighborhood). With every step, I am coming home to myself.

A wild soul morning is the very best sort. Already the cranky curmudgeon of me feels far away, left behind at the intersection of Rio Road and Highway 1, the last stop when heading south out of town into Big Sur.

Just ahead is the spot where I will step off the trail, amble down a little side track and find my perch above the shady stream amid the redwoods. There I'll slip off my shoes, and sit with pen and paper for an hour or so. Observing. Listening. Feeling.

So often I query in this weekly column, *to what will we give the gift of our attention?* And yet, a recent reading of the ever remarkable Mary Oliver has reminded me, "Attention without feeling... is only a report. An openness — an empathy — [is] necessary if the attention [is] to matter."

Carrying her words in my heart (as I do everywhere I go, having memorized several of her poems), my task on this wild soul morning is not simply to be outdoors in nature, good as that is; nor is it just to be quiet and observe what presents itself. Rather I am here to feel – deeply – and to sense myself interwoven once more with the soul and song of the world.

Put another way, lifting a line from one of Oliver's poems, "You have only to let the soft animal of your body / love what it loves."

❧ ❧ ❧

~ Part 2: Seeing

Amid the trees, the dry, herbaceous aromas of the lower canyon trail transform. Here the air is not only cooler by several degrees but suddenly tinged with mossy notes and a scent of green-tea, catapulting me to other places and other wanderings.

I slip off my daypack and settle on a wide, cut stump of an ancient redwood. The stream shines eight feet below me, gliding through lacy ferns and grey stones like a glistening snake, finding its way beneath a tangle of fallen logs and canyon detritus. Emerging, it forms a pool, the sort that would be deliciously tempting to wade into if the day was hot, but here within the shelter of the ravine and the tall, watchful trees, it's always cool.

Across the creek, the trail winds up the hillside above me. Occasionally the morning quietude is broken by the noise of people ascending the slope, conversing with each other, some of them huffing and puffing loudly.

Big Sur, especially the more easily accessible regions like this preserve, at this time of year is not really a place for deep solitude – especially on the weekend. Still, I am glad to be here. Like water in a dry land, nature feeds the soul.

Indeed, nature *is* the soul – the Soul of the World.

ఴ

Settling in, I am listening to the melody and distinct voices of the water – high notes, low notes – along with a scattering of birdsong in the green canopy overhead. Flying insects catch the filtered light, transformed into floating specks of gold that hover and dart, almost like faeries. My eye is drawn to the shifting reflection of dappled sunlight on the water – patterns dancing, impermanent, timeless. A pesky fly seems infatuated with my left earlobe, and repeatedly I shoo his noisy presence away.

Withdrawing a little black Moleskine journal from my rucksack, along with the trusty old fountain pen from France – newly repaired, its barrel no longer held with clear tape – I open to a blank, unlined page. Legs crossed, sitting upright, jotting down thoughts and observations, the familiar soft voice of the gold nib speaks as it scratches and glides across the thick drawing paper.

A good moment to savor, this.

It is the cusp of a new season and already the light is changing, diluted from summer's bold intensity; the temperature, while still warm, is also subtly decreasing. The autumn equinox is upon us and something unnamable flavors the air, almost like a whisper that causes me to shiver and smile with anticipation. A soft enchantment.

In the sky above the trees, the repeated shrill cry of a hawk pierces the canyon's quiet song, touching my soul.

Here is life, unhurried. Elemental. I inhale a deep breath, allowing myself to drop into my hip bones and slightly reposition my perch on the stump, senses dilating even wider and drinking deeply from what surrounds. With a twinge of regret, I realize that it is far too long since I spent a full day or night on the land, and like the yearning for a beloved, I feel the longing rise up in my chest like a strong, dark wave.

Come home, come home to the wild, barefoot stranger of yourself.

ↄ

Though I have left town (and mobile phone coverage) behind and crossed into Big Sur, and despite the gradual ascent along the canyon trail with my senses ajar, sloughing off my burdens and troubles, it takes a while to settle in to "nature" time. Almost like entering into a sitting meditation, there is a process of letting the mental noise drop away while encouraging the mind to become quiet. Some time is needed for modern-day filters to dissipate.

Similarly, it takes some time to begin to *see*. Textures. Relationships. Details and subtle variations. The infinite complexity of even a square inch here at my fingertips or toes is staggering. I could spend an hour looking at this fallen log littered with dried brown needles and never see it all – not even a fraction of it.

In our exquisite design, once the senses notice something and our brain registers it, when we next encounter that stimulus, we recognize it more quickly. It happens even faster the next time, and faster the time after that. Eventually, we hardly need to look at (or touch, smell, taste, etc.) a thing again in any curious sort of way; our brain fills in the picture largely from memory and pattern. *Oh, I'm in a shady coastal canyon with some ferns and redwoods and it's pretty.*

No longer novel or new, our experience and surroundings disappear into familiarity. In terms of seeing things, it's generally the newcomers, visitors, children, and artists who catch what others no longer register. The mystics, too, few as they are.

Georgia O'Keeffe, the American early modernist painter, used to say that people don't know how to see, to *really* see. She claimed it was part of the reason she painted flowers so large, so that people would finally notice them. "Nobody sees a flower really; it is so small. We haven't time, and to see takes time — like to have a friend takes time."

Even more time is required to *feel*, to shift from mental cognition and observation into an empathic, connected mode of being. A cellular response to our environment has guided mankind for millennia, a knowing in the heart through the direct perception of nature/environment. It is a wholistic mode of cognition – often wordless – that is distinctly different from the rational, linear, analytic mode that now dominates our world.

This empathic, feeling mode is instantaneous and utterly natural; it's simply a matter of making the shift from our heads down into our hearts that, like letting go of manmade time, can require a bit of effort for people.

❧

Usually, just when I'm really dropping into the depths of what surrounds me, when I am wide open (or at least much closer to that state than when I arrived), hovering at the point where I've relinquished clock time for nature time, it's time to depart.

If there's a gift in this irony, it is perhaps that when I am able to spend an extended period in "nature" – even a mere weekend – I open so widely that returning to our human, modern world is a painful assault: a rapid closing down again, drawing the shutters closed. Everything seems unnatural (because mostly it is). The return is generally a process that I find difficult, and the more expansive I have become, the more agonizing and sorrowful is the closing down.

Most people are so closed, so overstimulated and numbed from noise, television, radio, Internet, sirens, and loud voices, they don't realize it. Filters are locked firmly in place, sensory gating channels just barely open; we grow so habituated to this state that we don't even know what it means to be *open*. Unplugged from phone and laptop computer, and sitting beside a stream for a while, one might catch a little glimpse or taste of sensory dilation; or if able to walk through a park, one might feel a sense of openness spread through their core. Yet that's only the merest beginning.

I long to live where I can remain open, where my breath is full and unrestricted, where I hear the songs of trees, wind, water – a place where I find my inspiration, solace, and well-being.

Nature always brings me home to myself – my most authentic, expansive, best self – the one who is soft, flexible, receptive and aware. The one who is engaged in communion with the Larger Story, the one who beautifully embodies the Sacred Masculine. The one who *flows*.

ల

Perched above the little creek, time drifts downstream with the gracefully-moving water. Gazing upward into the mesh of green and brown conifer branches, an interwoven grille against a blue sky, as I allow my perspective and sense of depth to shift, I'm ever more at ease. With each breath, I am increasingly a part of the place I sit, less apart.

What a gift to be in this body savoring this exquisite moment. Yes, there's the usual ache in my knee as a minor distraction, but I am utterly content to be quietly observing and *feeling* – drawn into the deeper energies, observing that each thing is in relationship with everything else... me, included.

The longer I sit, the more I will open, and in that subtle drawing outwards, ever more I will see and feel.

Here, now, embraced by the shady arms of the canyon, I know one thing: *we are never separate*. Even in a state of expanded, heightened awareness, there is far more going on than we can imagine. Our job is simply to say "yes" to it and be open.

❧ ❧ ❧

~ Part 3: Return

Without fail, even after a relatively short immersion in the wild, I am transformed.

When I started up the dusty path from the trailhead, I felt constricted in a calcified shell of containment; irascible, burdened, and somewhat prickly (think, porcupine). Two hours later, when I emerge from the coastal canyon in Big Sur, I find myself ensconced in a bodysoul that feels soft and open, with feathered arms for flight.

Habitual filters, so necessary and unavoidable in our modern world, have fallen away. Things glimmer at the edge of my peripheral vision and awareness, spirits winking in and out. As my bare feet traverse the dry, uneven ground – sole meets soil meets soul – the very landscape has become animate, suggesting itself to me as shapes of animals, supernatural entities held in rock or tree. This, of course, is the *real* world, as it has always been: alive, breathing, fully intelligent and aware. Magical, even. We've simply stopped seeing it as such and become mostly blind.

An iridescent blue dragonfly zooms up to me and hovers near. Creature of both water and air, its long, narrow body like a thick blue needle floats suspended by a blur of gossamer wings. Somehow, these small messengers always remind me that everything in life is merely an illusion. As if the creature spoke, I hear a voice in my mind.

We are not separate. Life is simply a sea of energy... you, included.

எ

After a period of quiet sitting amid the tall evergreens with my senses ajar – listening, seeing, feeling, sensing – the mythic is near, beckoning me into the imaginal realm.

Imaginal does not mean imaginary; rather it is the world of archetypes, where the human psyche meets the Soul of the World. Describing the domain where the mythic and mundane interpenetrate each other, Henry Corbin first coined the term "imaginal" (he called it the *Mundus Imaginalis*), which was later employed by noted Jungian, James Hillman.

Entrance to this domain is gained by crossing the threshold of senses, open heart, and inspired imagination in moments when a door is left open – when the Mystery slides in unexpected to dance in the rooms of our shifting, expanded awareness. And because nature *is* the expanded, greater soul, a deep immersion in its realms is a powerful (perhaps unsurpassed) access route to the imaginal.

Thinking we can have it all, we've lost so much.

Disconnected from the natural world, holed up in our heads (while staring at a flat screen or handheld electronic device), we are estranged from a heart-centered cognition. Men, in particular. I speak of something more than simply *feeling*; a stepping away from the mental towards a more somato-emotional, intuitive way of knowing – an erudition that comes from the heart and our senses, from being deeply embodied in our bones and breath.

Like movement, respiration, and silence, nature invites us to expand; it offers the chance to remember that *the heart is a primary organ of perception*. To initiate the intuitive, wholistic mode of cognition, we have only to place our attention upon a thing (tree, bird, flower, person) and ask silently, how does it *feel*?

Immediately, there is a shift in our body. Breath deepens. The images, sensations, and affect arising in us with this sort of connection/communion form the real language of the world; something flows in, an awareness, a knowing in the heart that can be transmitted no other way. When we shift from thinking to feeling, from analyzing to simply observing and sensing, we slip casually across the threshold to an alluring, visceral realm that has mostly been lost to us.

❧

After my hour alongside the little flashing stream amid the watchful redwoods, casting the net of senses and heart wider with every breath, it is in the mythic, imaginal and fully animate world where I now find myself – a different realm than the identical looking one I passed through earlier. Drawn outwards, I am light and open. Diaphanous.

Edgewalker, remember who you are, the one who walks between worlds, following his heart's song.

I move differently now than when I arrived, something more feral than domesticated. How good it feels to be powerful, sensual, and free. No longer blocked and segmented, motor movement sequences through me in an effortless ripple and wave from the core. Rather than locked in the cage of my ribs, breath is expansive and free in the belly. Spine feels elongated, rusty hips somehow open and loose.

Somewhere amid the trees, I shed my heavy, limiting armor, and like some shape-shifter or shaman, became once again a graceful wildcat on softly padded paws.

Unhurried by manmade time, the humblest thing catches my attention – fading flower, sunbathing lizard, gnarled limbs of an oak – and seduces me with its marvelous, wordless beauty. This moment will never come again and I am fortunate enough to witness it.

What grace to celebrate and mirror back the extravagant creativity of the Cosmos. Such privilege to be in this body, a man with his heart wide open, smitten dumb and awestruck by the holy in everything. Is that not the very essence of embodying the Sacred Masculine? How remarkable and joyous that nature brings me to this place effortlessly, again and again... ever calling me home to myself and something much larger.

❧

Descending the coastal canyon, bare soles and soul appreciating the tactile connection with earth, feeling entirely in my element, I am slowly, reluctantly, returning to the manmade existence. Yet I am still composed of feathers and fur, scales and claws. Wings. A tail, perhaps. Threshold dweller at the edge of a continent where land meets sea and sky, I am fully myself – my best, most authentic, embodied and magical self. A wild soul enfolded by wild earth.

On the return, I always enjoy observing people's expressions when I pass them on the trail, the way their eyes glance down at my dusty, dirty feet. Or their comments, aloud to me or spoken to each other after I've passed.

"Wow, barefoot."

They notice my unclad feet mostly because they can't see my tail. Or glistening wings. They don't catch the wild hawk's gleam in my eye, or detect the catlike way I move, nor smell the wildness under my skin. We are blind and anesthetized to such things when we first emerge from the city, and for most folks, the filters never come off.

Repelled by the cloying, synthetic scent of fabric softener on their clothes, nostrils flared to the autumn air, I move past them with feral grace and keep heading down the trail.

❧

I can hear the afternoon with its awaiting work at home calling to me, a distant drone and vaguely metallic voice, but I'm in no hurry to answer. All in good time. Even with the small rucksack on my back, I feel so light and unencumbered that it almost seems that something is missing.

Then I notice: I've left my shoes back amid the redwoods.

The mirth in this is simply delightful, and laughter bubbles up like a spring from somewhere deep inside. As I turn around and head back up to the great trees, to the little side path leading down to the stream where I had been sitting on the great old stump, I cannot help but be amused.

Something of myself always gets left when I depart the wild, natural realms and return to everyday life, but today what I've lost is something a bit weightier than just my spirit.

I am still chuckling when I find my sandals, right where I left them, waiting for me. I pick them up but don't put them on, stashing them inside my pack, and then once more head back down the trail. Smiling. Musing on the things we carry and the things we leave behind.

౿ఎ

On any quest – whether a mythic journey, a long process of self-discovery, a modern day 'vision quest', even a weekend workshop – the one who returns is not the same as the one who went out.

Whether or not we find the talisman we seek – even if that is only an elusive sense of peace and quiet – the very process of severance from the rote and familiar, then venturing into the unknown and the experience that greets us there, *changes* us.

To what will we give the gift of our attention?

Still expansive and stitched of silken moth wings, I am different now. Strangely whole again. Fully human *and* something just a bit more.

Approaching the wide mouth of the arid, lower canyon, I hear the noise of the highway as I nearly simultaneously catch the briny scent and muffled voice of the sea. I am emerging from one realm into another.

As always happens back at the car, I experience the momentarily strange sense of being confined, surrounded by synthetic materials. I want to immediately roll down the windows, but at the same time I strongly desire to be shielded from the steady, rolling noise of the highway. And so it begins: the pulling in and gradual closing-down.

In the hours and days ahead, even in the sanctuary of a little cottage near the sea, in my deliberately constructed life of soulful rituals, the modern day amnesia will slowly creep over me. Senses will dull and once again I'll forget the full, non-domesticated, sensual wildness of who I am. That is, until the restlessness under my skin, the wild soul, urges me back out into the trees or onto a sage-covered mesa, where I wake up again and remember. Re-wilding myself.

That's why I need to live on the edge of wild places, at the threshold between worlds, so I can just slip out and disappear among the quietly singing trees and come home to myself – dancing naked and yipping at the great luminous pearl of moon.

Remember who you are, edgewalker, a wild, barefoot soul with wings on your arms.

No shoes required.

❧ ❧ ❧

Shadows and Healing
(November 2016)

O utside my window, the branches of a coconut palm sway in a warm, coastal breeze like graceful, serrated green fans.

For the past two weeks I have been in Honolulu, helping my mate prepare for the 36th annual Hawaii International Film Festival, in his role as Executive Director. Here in the islands, as I sit and gaze at the azure waters of the Pacific, autumn on the mainland with its cool air and falling, painted leaves, seems a world away, like something from a book or a movie. And yet as removed as this emerald archipelago generally feels, even here the US presidential election and its aftermath weighs like a heavy cloud or shadow.

Indeed, *shadow* seems an appropriate word in many ways, as the repressed elements of America's collective consciousness – a tsunami of anger, fear, racism, bigotry and greed – now rush forward and sweep onto the national stage. For two days following the election, I chose to abstain from any media news feed. My only exception was Facebook, where I briefly glanced at some of my friends' posts, and selectively read a few insightful and inspiring pieces by people whom I admire or *follow*, or that my friends follow and have shared. And "shadow" was used in nearly all the posts I encountered.

ॐ

Rarely do I speak or write about anything overtly political, and I refrain from posting my political views or opinions (which are decidedly "green," progressive, and Earth-centric) on social media. Partly this is because I think politics, in general, is reductionist; us versus them, red versus blue, Democrat against Republican, or Conservative versus Labour versus Green, etcetera. While it is convenient to use such labels, what we are actually witnessing and attempting to describe is the interplay (and conflict) of differing levels of the intersubjective agreements we might call *worldviews*, which reflect a framework of value systems applied to sociocultural evolution.

Cultures evolve through a distinct set of stages, from lower to higher, as the societies and individuals evolve and integrate within them; each set of values is a response to solving the problems of the previous stage. On a level of politics, people will embrace a party or group that reflects their worldview's particular level of development. The inherent challenge is that we cannot understand or grasp a reality or worldview more evolved or expansive than our own current level. Until our own circle of identity shifts (say from *egocentric* to *ethnocentric*, or to *nature* or *world-centric*), we simply haven't the capacity to embrace more expansive worldviews than our current one. It is literally beyond us.

As I wrote in a post a few weeks ago: "*In certain respects, our personal growth resembles rings of a tree; we become larger and more expansive than younger versions of ourselves, still containing those smaller circumferences but also exceeding them. At each stage, we may or may not even acknowledge that we are growing, and we don't yet perceive the wider, larger Self and worldview that we will later embody. We might look back and detect the earlier phases and versions passed through and outgrown, but not yet the larger ones to come.*"

Hence, a tribal culture in Afghanistan or traditional society in Iraq cannot leap ahead to a democracy; there are several evolutionary stages that *must* be navigated and passed through first, both on individual and collective levels. Closer to home, the conservatives simply cannot understand most liberals or progressives – let alone the Greens – because their worldview has not yet expanded to the wider, more inclusive circles of identity.

In a nuclear age and time of global shift, certainly it matters who holds the reins of a country, but ultimately each of us must look within to find and create the change we seek. Amid the collective despair of the moment, we can easily become fixated on the idea that America's national election is the most compelling and urgent story, especially for those of us who care deeply about human rights, the planet, and all its denizens. Yet the Larger Story of our collective evolution is bigger than this – much bigger – and rather than looking for salvation in a leader (or anyone else), the most transforming journey remains an inner, spiritual one. When our personal growth progresses and unfurls – very often through a soul crisis – it becomes transpersonal; collectively, our individual evolution (which *must* include "shadow work" and facing the demons in our inner darkness) also realigns the cultural worldview, nudging it slowly along the upward spiral. Too slowly, it seems.

Opinions of politics and evolution aside, I believe that most of modern Western culture, particularly America, suffers from a deep soul sickness. Evidenced by our addiction to money and technology, along with a pervasive ennui and lack of meaning in life, it is caused in considerable part by an absence of the sacred, alongside our pathological disconnection from what we might call *wildness* and Nature (despite that nature exists everywhere, right down to our cells and soul). An unwavering faith in science and "progress" has given us many answers and explanations, along with an increased comfort and ease, yet it has also robbed us of much of the magic and mystery that once underpinned human life, while turning the living world into merely an array of "resources" to be exploited.

Perhaps it seems overly simplistic to say that capitalism, the Industrial Revolution, and an extractive, corporate economy have resulted in the breakdown of society's fabric, but many experts worldwide have persuasively argued exactly this view, and I am inclined to agree with them. Certainly it is nothing new for people to feel disenfranchised, ignored, powerless, angry, and disillusioned with their lot in life, and to express the related feelings as hate, bigotry, chauvinism, greed, or violence – acting out the lowest level of human behavior. Yet the fact that so many people are choosing to embrace such traits and expressions in order to espouse and support their values, reveals just how deep our collective Shadow really is.

℘

Most indigenous, traditional people and cultures believe in the presence of spirits, and that malevolent ones can enter a person and take over in the form of "possession." Traditional healers, medicine men, *curanderos*, and shamans use a variety of different methods for removing the foreign entity, employing spiritual or energetic measures as well as various plant medicines to literally purge the bad element from the body – as with ayahuasca ceremonies, where *la purga* (usually vomiting or diarrhea) caused by the medicine, constitutes an important part of the healing process.

On my own healing journey, I believe that the source of our woes is much more complex than simply evil spirits (though I know firsthand that they exist), pathogens, genes, incomplete psychological development, trauma, or energetic imbalance ... or even politics. If only it were as easy as giving everyone a powerful emetic and/or purgative, or performing a "soul retrieval" or working with plant medicines, to restore us to some semblance of well-being and sanity.

Individually or culturally, there is no cure for our Shadow other than looking at what we have ignored, repressed or locked away as unacceptable. We must gaze truthfully into the mirror, accepting that the darkness or ignorance is not simply *them* – whomever we perceive those to be – for each of us is both darkness and light. As C.G. Jung commented when speaking of the Shadow, "I myself am the enemy that must be loved."

Our society is very broken, rife with despair as its shadow runs amok. Yet as a healer and an "evolutionary," I know it is only crisis that forces us to change, especially on a large scale. *Evolution happens at the fringes, never in the status quo.* We have only to look at nature, history, and the story of the cosmos to see that crisis is *always* the catalyst for previously inconceivable leaps forward in development. And this great upwelling of collective shadow, along with our impending crisis of climate change accompanied by the breakdown of globalization, may be the factors that push us past the tipping point into a necessary – and ultimately healing – shift.

In the meantime, millions of people currently find themselves in a state of shock and grief, both of which have real effects and repercussions on the bodysoul. Any overwhelming stimulus, especially one that seems potentially life-threatening, whether on an individual or world scale, triggers a traumatic response in our autonomic nervous system. As Americans now come to grips with a reality that was previously unimaginable, we must find ways to allow the trauma – for that is exactly what has happened for many on Election Night – to discharge, unwind, and sequence through, so that it doesn't remain frozen and held in the body. [Post-Traumatic Stress Disorder (PTSD) is actually previous trauma still held immobilized in the nervous system, and the right impetus or stimulus again triggers a well-patterned "fight or flight" response.]

Yet one of the ways we can begin to emerge from shock is to find appropriate ways to discharge the held energy in our nervous system. Crying might be a good start for accessing the grief, followed by exploring movement and sound, and seeking ways to put that grief (or outrage) into meaningful action. A woman I know "virtually"–whose hauntingly soulful music I've praised in a previous SAJ post, "The Wild Songstress: Daring to Be Yourself"–recently wrote on Facebook and to her followers: *"I will feel the grief and continue to sing, wail, drum, and pray for this great world, for this breathtakingly beautiful land, for indigenous people and their legacies of wisdom, for the scurrying-swimming-galloping-flitting-soaring-innocent things, for the humble ones who choose to serve rather than dominate, and for those who grieve in this time for the many, many pains of this world..."*

I find her words to be beautiful, insightful, and wise, for we can best help grief to heal if we actually allow it to *move*, rather than remaining held. And along with some form of embodied movement and sound, we can turn to Nature, for it is about the only thing big enough and "real" enough to hold the depths of sadness (or rage) as we work through to reclaim the heart of Love.

☙

Indeed, Mother Earth is the larger story that holds and supports us all. Almost exactly a year ago, in a SAJ post called "Kneel and Kiss the Earth" I wrote:

"Whenever I am out of sorts – blue, restless, unwell, disappointed – I need to touch the earth, feel it soft and yielding beneath my footsteps. Always it is the embrace that I must return to. Tell me what you love, *it breathes voicelessly as the wind rustles the surrounding trees,* and I will remind you who you are."

Just a week later, following the attacks in Paris, my heart heavy for a place that is very dear to me, I shared: *"It is good and right to shed tears for the world, I think, but may we weep also for its staggering beauty. Everywhere. And if you cannot find beauty in what surrounds you, go in search of it – or create it with your hands and heart, and then give it away selflessly. Freely. Madly. Even if it's just a song. A poem. A story. Perhaps a garden. Or a simple supper for your beloved..."* (excerpted from "A Heart Open to the World: Finding Beauty," SAJ 2015)

Those words still hold true for me, perhaps even more today than when I penned them, now seeing America so bitterly divided. Friend, a larger story enfolds us than the headlines splashed across the newspapers or on TV, and while surely these are challenging times, I continue to say that the path remains inward – into our shadows to unearth and embrace the heart of compassion and empathy, and to carry it back out into the world, offering what each of us may bring in service to something greater. May the journey be a healing one. For all of us.

Blessed be.

❧ ❧ ❧

A Simple Supper: An Impromptu Risotto
(October 2014)

I'm back in the kitchen.

Mind you, *l'espace cuisine* in my little artist's studio in coastal California is more like a sailboat's galley. It's decidedly a one-person space. The cooking alcove – which closes off behind folding wooden doors – does have a certain charm, and it feels very Old World to me. The impression is generated not only by the snug dimensions but the narrow, Euro-style gas stove/cooker similar to what I had in France, and the way-too-small-to-be-American fridge; it's also the old-fashioned wood cabinets, low beamed ceiling, the two vintage art-deco glass shades shaped like tulip bulbs, and the stained glass doors of the dish cupboard. If I wasn't looking out at a New World landscape, I could almost be back somewhere in Europe. *Almost.*

A cozy little space, this. There are moments when working at the small tiled counter between the sink and the stove, feeling cramped, that I somewhat feel like I am back at culinary school in Paris and trying to create the day's cuisine (or patisserie). Except that I'm not elbow to elbow with fellow students in chef's jackets, all wearing our silly caps and *cravat* tied around our perspiring necks – and the kitchen temperature is not sweltering from ten ovens ablaze. Also, there's no pressure to get my creation done right or in a certain (read, French) way. Too, there's the fact that I'm looking out a window to an ocean view framed by gracefully windswept evergreens.

Honestly, the small gas range with its four burners is a thing of joy for me. In my nomadic wanderings and rented houses, I have long since resigned my fate where ovens are concerned, and I've suffered through far too many electric cookers, new and old. I detest them all, even the modern flat ones. Induction, too. All things being equal, I'll always choose the house/kitchen with the gas range, thank you.

As if it were not good fortune enough to be in this charming little, oceanside sanctuary for a stretch of my journey, it has a gas stove, and I'm generally inspired to cook something on it nightly.

The other day, after a long morning spent working on Book 2 and then several hours seeing bodywork clients, I came home feeling utterly tired and hungry, which is seldom a good combination for inspiration of any sort. I had intended to do some grocery shopping after work, but when that moment finally arrived I decided that I simply wasn't up to the task. I trusted that I could rummage around at home and put *something* together with a few odds and ends.

The day was misty and cool, a definite note of autumn in the air, and as evening descended in soft tones and hues, I wanted something warm and comforting. Opening the storage cupboard, I considered the various glass jars of grains, pulses, beans, and whatnot. Briefly I eyed the three usual contenders: quinoa, millet, and buckwheat – all of which are alkalizing for the body rather than acid-forming, and in the Ayurvedic healing approach, each of them warming and balancing for a cool and damp Kapha constitution such as mine. I sighed, uninspired. Behind the front row, pushed up close against the stone-ground polenta, the plump, pearly arborio rice softly called out, *You want risotto.*

Rich, warm, creamy and comforting, the classic rice dish always seems like perfect cool weather fare to me. I pulled the jar from behind the others and set it on the diminutive countertop.

I opened the fridge to see what sort of options might be to hand, and to be sure that I had an onion. There is usually a knob of Parmesan to be found (along with a wedge or two of various cheeses). There is always butter in the house, and wine – a lingering outcome of attending culinary school in Paris. Nigel Slater, one of my favourite British cookery authors, writes in one of his dear-to-my-heart books, "I get a bit twitchy if there's not wine in the house." Amen, Nigel, but I'll still chalk it up to having lived in France.

Considering the broth required, I briefly hesitated. I haven't cooked a chicken since being in this recently acquired studio, so there was no proper stock to hand. At home in Hawaii, I keep homemade chicken broth in the freezer, a stash that gets replenished regularly. Not here. A couple of organic vegetable bouillon cubes would have to suffice. (For the record, only the "veggie" ones are any good; the others taste artificial and impart an unwelcome, cloying flavor to any dish. Please don't bother with them.) A risotto cooked with veggie stock, even a vegetable broth made from scratch at home, never quite has the unctuous, velvety satin finish of one crafted with a proper chicken broth. Tired and hungry, I decided there was no sense being fussy or proud about the stock; it would only be me eating it, after all. Veggie bouillon cubes then. Sorted.

In autumn, I'm fond of butternut squash risotto, sometimes spiked with pungent sage. Or a risotto of roasted beets. I've been known to cook both diced butternut and beets, separately, and either combine them in the finished dish or split the nearly cooked rice into two pots, adding beets to one and squash to the other, and then serving the ensuing crimson and golden-orange risottos side by side in a dish, which looks *stunning*. Alas that I had neither of those good ingredients in my empty kitchen. I peered once more into the barren wasteland of the fridge, as if something might magically appear to give my meager risotto any extra pizazz. No such luck. Empty is... empty.

Sitting lonely on the top shelf of the fridge, however, was the squat, hinged-lid glass jar with the remainder of the Moroccan green *charmoula* from two evenings before: a bold, gutsy sauce of garlic, capers, anchovy, toasted cumin, black pepper, a pinch of cayenne, olive oil, and fresh green herbs that I had pounded up using my Provençal mortar and pestle. (The North African sauce had topped a filet of pan-fried local rockfish, alongside some fresh green beans.) I considered it for a moment, tasting the flavors in my mind, and decided, *why not*. Risotto in our house stopped being anything close to "traditional" at least fifteen years ago, and given that we don't eat pasta, I value the classic rice dish for its versatility and ability to gracefully incorporate a wide range of ingredients (not necessarily all at the same time) – even if what finds its way into the pot is seldom *classic*.

I turned on some music by a favorite female jazz vocalist, lit the various pillar candles on the stone hearth, then stepped back into *l'espace cuisine* and poured a glass of white wine for myself. I plunked a couple bouillon cubes into several cups of water to bring to the boil, set the bamboo cutting board on the small counter space and chopped the lone, organic onion that had been lurking forlornly in the fridge drawer. Cut into tidy squares, I tipped it into the pan where a bit of olive oil and a small pat of butter were warming, whereupon a pleasant sizzle and familiar, enticing aroma rose up to greet my senses.

After the onion softened to a glistening translucence, I added the arborio (*carnaroli* makes far better risotto but good luck finding any that is organically grown). Stirring for a minute or two to coat the grains with the hot oil and butter, I added a gurgling, happy slosh of the Oregon Pinot Gris, and as the rice absorbed the wine, I settled contentedly into the easy ritual of adding a ladle full of broth, one at a time, stirring each until it absorbed before adding the next.

I've done this for so many years, making risotto in a wide variety of pots and pans and kitchens, there is something deeply comforting, calming, even meditative about it. When my mate and I have resided in cooler, temperate locales, risotto has often been a weekly supper in the cold months of the year. It is a dish so deeply ingrained in my bodymind that it requires almost no conscious thought, yet still deserves my attention and care – appreciating the goodness of each element that goes into it, scattering quiet blessings over the steaming surface as I work, and stirring them in.

With genuine tiredness in my body, I grated the lump of Parmesan and gazed out the little porthole of window, noting the shifting hues of the sky and the cove's waters as evening descended. A long day already, it seemed, but comforting to be in the kitchen preparing a simple supper to feed my bodysoul in a welcoming, nourishing manner.

On a whim, I turned from stirring the rice and opened the spice cupboard. Peering inside at the few, select offerings I keep on hand, I flirted briefly with adding a good dash of *pimenton ahumado*, my favorite Spanish smoked paprika (they range in heat and pungency), for a hint of intrigue alongside the herby charmoula. What caught my eye instead was the small jar of Spanish saffron threads. I tossed a good pinch of the precious russet stamens into the hot rice, where they quickly began to bleed their glorious golden hue, and that indescribable, hypnotic and ancient scent that is *azafran* rose up to seduce me.

When the bright yellow, fragrant grains had absorbed all the broth and its texture was right, I dumped in the grated Parmesan, a small knob of butter, and then four heaping tablespoons – all that remained – of the herb charmoula, and stirred it together. The now-yellow rice was flecked with green, and given the alchemy of heat, the garlic and other ingredients in the Moroccan sauce offered up another intoxicating Mediterranean aroma, dancing and swirling with that of the saffron.

I transferred a good amount of creamy rice to one of the deep French bowls I have here at the cottage, and dusted it with a wee bit of the Parmesan. Gathering a soupspoon and linen napkin, I carried my modest meal and cutlery outdoors to the little rusting bistro table in front of the cottage. I made a quick return for a light jacket and my current favorite scarf, along with the glass of wine, and then sat down to my simple supper as it steamed fragrantly.

The flashing sea rolled and churned in a timeless low chant, its briny scent wafting through the shapely trees, and I opened all senses wide to the quiet evening around me. Counting my blessings. Missing my partner and dogs. Appreciating the marine air and beauty that enfolds me here at this magical poet's cottage, content in my cherished solitude, and oh so ready for a bit of supper at the end of a long day.

Tasting the risotto, my eyes rolled back in my head. *Oh la la,* it was just *that good* – the subtle but exotic note of the saffron underscoring the herb flavors of the charmoula, coupled with the creamy warmth of the rice. Bold and lusty, like a culinary hustler. I ate it slowly, savoring each mouthful, marveling once again that a meal so modest, frugal even, could be this deeply satisfying. And though it was an entirely different taste, setting, and season, the gustatory moment was somehow not unlike the one I experienced a few months earlier with the fresh goodness from the roadside stand, and shared in "A Bowl of Peas."

How do we feed the soul? This is an ongoing question and exploration in these posts – and my own life. I have written repeatedly about the act of cooking itself (you can find those posts jumbled under the Slow Food category of the archive), how being in the kitchen can offer its own soulful nourishment even apart from the actual food. Most of us tend to view preparing a meal as a necessary task rather than a creative ritual, or wish that someone else would do it for us, especially when we are tired and uninspired. Yet choosing to commit to an act that nourishes us in some primary way, whether literal or metaphorical, is a keystone for a life of deeper meaning, appreciation, and contentment.

Maybe cooking isn't one of those soulful rituals for you, gentle reader, but here's hoping that you find *something* in your day, even when you are weary and lackluster – perhaps most especially then – that opens your senses and feeds your bodysoul in some deep, essential manner. We can exist on very little (and most of us have way too much), but only when we are *nourished* do we thrive. Let your focus be on nourishment... and savoring. Like gratitude, it can transform your moment and the day.

Whenever possible, may you share such goodness with others. If we touch just one life in a positive fashion, made someone else's day a bit brighter through what we bring and offer, we have succeeded in a key aspect of life's journey. And if bodymind and senses are expansive in the process of that giving, we move closer to a deep state of *ensoulment.* And grace.

May we all be fed on such a deep level.

❧ ❧ ❧

In the Realm of Falcons: A New Year's Hike
(January 2015)

I knew the trail would be crowded on New Year's Day but I went regardless.

After a quiet morning at my cottage studio, ensconced in the southerly window seat, watching a calm blue sea through the ornate framework of tangled Monterey cypress trees, a cup of tea beside me and a book on my lap, I decided that I would go for a wander. Despite the tranquility of the scene, I could feel a buzzing energy beneath my skin, a nearly tingling restlessness of a bodysoul ready to stretch, move and walk. What could be better than to begin the New Year with a good ramble on a bright sunny day?

I stashed a few essentials in my small daypack – water, almonds, a couple of clementines, my red bandana, soft shell jacket, fountain pen and notebook – strapped on my walking sandals, hopped in the car, and drove just south of the Carmel Highlands to Garrapata State Park. Sure enough, Highway 1 was crowded with parked cars for a long distance in both directions.

Garrapata is close enough to town that it nearly always seems to be busy (though not nearly so much as Point Lobos, which is positively overrun and loved to death), and normally I simply pass it by, heading for somewhere less trafficked, deeper in the heart of Big Sur. I guessed that the crowds might be thinner if I drove further, say to Andrew Molera State Park, or down to Julia Pfeiffer Burns State Park, but somehow I didn't feel inclined to go that far or spend much time in the car.

My desire was to be in a redwood canyon, amid the presence of those noble trees that I adore, so I decided to make my way along the busy Soberanes Canyon trail rather than the Rocky Ridge climb overlooking the sea. No matter which path I chose, given all the traffic of a holiday, it would not be a walk for solitude. I tried to ignore the noisiness of groups of teenagers on the trail, along with the obvious (read, oblivious) city folk who were clearly out of their element but animatedly having a good time; frequently I stepped aside to let groups and families pass on their noisy way down the narrow trail.

I endeavored to simply appreciate the beauty of the alluring canyon with its evergreen trees and happily singing stream, but I found myself pushing on faster than I would normally stroll on one of my soulful rambles. Perhaps if I get up a bit higher, I'll leave some of the casual day strollers behind, I thought.

In the green confines of the canyon it was cool enough that I wore my goosedown vest, though I soon warmed sufficiently from the climb that I didn't really need it. I opened all senses wide to the tall conifers and their canopy overhead, a notable presence around and above, feeling a sense of delight in my leg and gluteal muscles working on the steady ascent. The trail was too busy and steep to stop and linger with any hope of quiet or solitude, though in a dozen places I felt a yearning to return there on some midweek winter day when the canyon would be more tranquil. I was new to this hike, and as I climbed I toyed with the idea of heading up to a ridge – surely such a lookout is where it would lead – where I might get a good view of the Pacific and find a serene place to sit. Perhaps write a bit.

On and on I climbed, thinking each rise would reveal the crest that I wanted, perhaps a lower hillside amid the high ridgelines still towering above me. Yet each section of trail yielded only another stretch of climbing. Near the top of the redwood canyon, following an athletic family with four teenage girls, I watched them ascend the steep slope of chaparral, separated in distance and moving according to their respective musculature, speed and constitution. From my perspective, it seemed the handsome, super-fit dad had reached a summit, where he stood waiting for the rest of his clan to catch up.

I'll just go up there to the top, I thought, huffing and puffing. Surely it's a good view.

By the gods, the short distance proved remarkably challenging, and I halted repeatedly to catch my breath and rest my dodgy knees that groaned loudly from the effort. Just ahead of me, the mother ascended easily behind her youngest daughter who moved along with hiking poles while clearly uninspired, encouraging her repeatedly.

"Just keep your eyes on the prize, honey. This is the steepest part. It's *much* easier after this."

I drew my own encouragement from her ongoing stream of positive talk.

As we collectively stopped for a moment, I said aloud to the mom standing ten feet away, "Climbing with you, I feel like I have my own private hiking coach."

"Great!" she beamed with bright eyes and cheerleader enthusiasm. "Glad I could help you a bit! This is probably the most difficult hike on the peninsula, but totally worth it."

Climbing on, I chuckled to myself. Naturally in my naiveté I picked the most challenging ascent. Sort of like deciding to write a book, I sighed.

Scrambling up the sandy trail, my mind flashed to the Superstition Mountains in Arizona, one of my first backpacking trips as an apprentice guide for wilderness-based rites of passage, where I followed my co-apprentice, an experienced wilderness man, off the trail, down a steep and rocky slope, and then up a challenging stream bed. A dozen times I was ready to turn back, to find an easier route, yet I struggled on. Grumbling. Ascending the backcountry canyon, we eventually found ourselves in an unimaginable oasis: a high ravine with clear pools, a primeval temple of great sycamore trees and jagged red cliffs, utterly pristine and magical. Had I chosen an easier way or stuck to the main path, I would never have encountered something so deeply alluring.

℘

Looking out over the rugged reaches of Big Sur as I paused to catch my breath, the day's ascent seemed an apt metaphor for my journey the past years: struggling on towards an unknown destination, going much farther than I had originally planned, but at a certain point knowing that I would push on to the end and see it through, no matter what.

When I finally reached what I previously imagined as the top or summit, where Mr. Fit and his daughters had been waiting but were now gone, I found the trail winding on, a long dusty snake slithering up toward a yet higher ridgeline. The path was significantly less steep than the 32° grade I had just ascended for the past 0.4 mile, but I laughed with weary exhaustion. Bugger.

I gazed back over the canyon from which I had just climbed, toward the southerly coastal summits draped with trailing wisps of pale cloud, and west towards the blue sea ablaze with a great white ribbon of sunlight. All the landscape shimmered green from the recent rains, and everywhere I turned my eyes I felt the subtle sense of renewal, a welcome change after the long months of drought and thirst.

Were the slope more forgiving or welcoming, I could have rested there for an hour and been utterly content, gazing towards the Ventana wilderness away south.

Yet I knew from the mother's encouragement of her struggling daughter that somewhere up ahead sat a bench (where they would all meet up and take a family photo), and I decided that I would simply go on. The bench would be my victory celebration, after which I would make my way back down, having already gone much farther and higher than planned.

When I finally reached the ridge top, well above the tree line, wide open and carpeted with wild green grass, I was buffeted by the cool winds, rapidly cooling the moisture of my perspiration-soaked shirt. The cliffs and summits of Big Sur are often obscured in fog, but the view all along the coastline stretched clear, stitched loosely with a few white cotton clouds.

I cannot say it was exactly tranquil at the summit, not with a dozen or more people laughing and talking as they milled about the various vista spots of jumbled boulders, but the stunning panorama and sense of accomplishment from the trek made the climb worthwhile. I hadn't come for quiet *soul time* (though I would have welcomed it, as I always do), not on a national holiday, but rather for a good ramble, and in that I had succeeded brilliantly.

What a curious episode of grace, I mused, that just at the most difficult part of the climb, when I was ready to turn back, I found myself alongside the mother and daughter, encouraged to go on towards an unknown destination despite the great difficulty. Grace, indeed.

༄

I took off my walking sandals to be barefoot on the cool earth, strolled to the edge and gazed out over the blue Pacific, some 1850 feet below me. Suddenly a kestrel rose up on the wind's current and hovered just a dozen feet away, russet wings rapidly beating the air as he hung suspended in the breeze, his keen eyes scanning the green slope below. In a flash, my heart soared alongside him and the tiredness of my body seemed to fall away. I've not seen a kestrel or falcon – nor had such a dramatic hike – since residing in Spain four years ago.

In Andalucía, a pair of kestrels lived somewhere near our whitewashed, stone farmhouse on the hillside amid the gnarled olive trees, and I frequently spied them when I was out wandering the groves, hiking, or even just standing on the terrace, gazing out over the *campo* toward the turquoise wedge of the near-distant Mediterranean. I always felt graced when they appeared.

I stood for several minutes watching the small falcon swoop and dive, then hover again, hunting the steep hillside until he disappeared. For the briefest of moments, I imagined the tattooed wings on my forearms pulsed ever so slightly, dreaming of flight.

Walking along the westerly edge of the summit, as I prepared to descend the Rocky Ridge trail, thus forming a loop back down to the coastline far below, the kestrel swept up and hovered close at hand, bold and unafraid of human presence.

"Hello, beauty," I smiled.

He plunged, veered swiftly left, and vanished into the canyon, leaving me once again graced by his presence. It felt oddly like an affirmation of sorts. A wild blessing. A welcome touch from the soul of the world.

My trip down through the steep chaparral was slow going in places, the incline being sandy and a bit treacherous, though there is little danger of going off a cliff. The vast majority of hiking mishaps happen on the descent, and despite my precaution, the grip of my Keen sandals was insufficient on the loose gravel and I took a short slide, using my hand as an emergency brake, which didn't fare well for the skin on my palm. Using spit to wash away the grit and some of the blood, I wrapped my peeled palm in the red bandana I had stashed in my rucksack and kept going, even more slowly. Thankfully I had landed backward on my left ankle, plantar-flexed against the rocky ground rather than twisted out to the side and severely spraining it.

The bright disc of sun sinking down to kiss the welcoming sea, finally I found myself at the bottom of the long hill, bundled up against the cool breeze, walking back to my car parked on the noisy highway, feeling well-tired but happy with my unplanned adventure to the Big Sur ridge top. With its steep climb, the five-mile loop offered a solid workout for the body, and even with so many others on the trail, I felt deeply nourished in my soul from the wild beauty of my surroundings. I suspected that my quadriceps (and perhaps my calves) would tomorrow have something to say about the climbing and descent. So be it. I would go home to a hot shower and a warming bit of New Year's Day soup, perhaps even a glass of nice bubbly.

I smiled at it all, thinking that the trek and metaphor would make a good and fitting epitaph for my life:

Inspired by nature and wild beauty, he went much farther than planned or imagined. The climb was worth the effort.

Friend, whether you set out to climb a ridge summit, or perhaps find yourself struggling up an unexpectedly steep, slippery slope at a stretch of your life, or simply going farther along a passage than you anticipated, may you meet unexpected grace and guides along the way. Remember that angels almost always show up in human form. (That said, falcons or other wild ones are entirely plausible disguises.) And when you finally reach the summit – or simply arrive back at home, exhausted – may your heart open wide, whatever the view may be, and you possess a fuller sense of yourself for having made the challenging journey.

✌ ✌ ✌

Candlebright

(September 2014)

Aman sits in the dark window, bundled in a light grey jacket and a blue Parisian scarf wrapped around his neck. By the light of a lone beeswax taper that flickers nearby on the table, his unruly and uncombed hair shines silver though his face is that of a man in his forties. Awake long before the dawn, in a circle of illumination cast by the candle, he writes with fountain pen in a notebook, a cup of tea on a saucer beside him growing tepid while it listens to the scratching of gold nib upon paper.

Summoned from dreams by a strange call in the darkness, he rises, disoriented at first. Naked in the dark womb of the cottage, he stands at the bifurcated door with its upper panes of old glass, gazing out at moonlit waters of the cove and gnarled trees outlined as shadow beings. Listening. No fog or mist lingers about the eaves, the world is only a dark crystal into which to skry.

Opening the door, he steps onto the cool stones of the small covered porch. Still nude in the cool air that brings his whole body alive and tingling, the murmuring low voice of the rolling sea greets him with briny breath, mingled with a fragrant, vaguely lemony scent of Monterey cypress trees. But for the timeless chant of ocean, a deep quietude and stillness holds all in a realm of glimmering shadows and thin moonlight.

The man retreats into the relative warmth of the cottage. He is tempted to return to the cozy comfort of bed but realizes that, once again, he has been curiously invited to greet this morning in the briefly numinous moment when two worlds touch. Reluctantly, he pulls on clothes from the chair, neatly placed there the night before when he undressed for sleep. Clad more warmly, he steps again outdoors in the moonlight and walks slowly with bare feet down to the circle of trees at the edge of the southerly cove.

The ring of Dancers. Seven windswept Monterey cypress trees that gracefully root down into earth and stone, rising up in timeless, evergreen song. Behind him, the warm glow of the candle in the window illuminates the cottage, a small, bright beacon in the surrounding darkness. The man steps into the deeply shadowed enclave as if it were a druid's grove, a place humming with power, secrets, and an ancient wordless song. Gathered round with furrowed, grey arms entwined, the trees are silhouetted against the flashing liquid silver of the sea.

Welcome, earth son.

His eyes scan the surrounding shadows, senses wide, feeling and listening. Mountain lions are not uncommon here, and the hours of dawn and dusk are hunting ones. Yet there is little real danger; for a great cat, there exists an abundance of far easier prey than an adult human. He shrugs away the cold tickle of fear and his projections, and raises his arms to the canopy overhead woven of lacy charcoal mesh.

"If it's my time to go, it's my time to go," he says silently. "For now, I celebrate the moment, the coming dawn, and the mystery of you that is everywhere."

Holy... holy.

Speaking aloud to the darkly liminal forms that surround, he offers one of the poems carried in his heart, a way to greet the morning though the eastern sky is not yet light. The golden chariot of day remains some ways off yet, chasing the alluring moon.

Dance, he hears a voice say.

In the ring of Dancers, he begins to dance. Slowly. Stiffly. Limbs move, energy flows, breath increases, bare soles tromp and shuffle amid the cool dirt and sticky shedding of the cypresses. After a few minutes, the man settles back to simply standing. His body feels awake and alive, senses further open to the song of the world.

Bowing to the circle of trees, he walks back toward the flickering light of the cottage windows.

On the fireplace hearth, a second candle, a tall pillar, flickers. The man ignites a stick of resinous piñon incense from the American Southwest, places the smoldering taper in its holder, and crosses to the small galley of a kitchen. He switches on a single light above the gas stove, a shapely tulip of antique frosted glass. Electric incandescence floods the space, causing his wide brown eyes to contract and squint. Still wearing his jacket and scarf, he stirs a small pan of warming water and cereal grains – oats, quinoa, amaranth – that will yield a warm breakfast on this cool morning.

The cottage is silent, so too the world outside the sheltering walls and roof. He appreciates the meditation of stirring the pot with a wooden spoon over the blue flame. The gentle and mindful energy keeps with how he begins the day – a hushed and magical meeting of darkness and light, tending the soul at the misty threshold of earth, sea, and sky.

I am quietly old fashioned, the man observes, and the thought bestows a sense of gentle satisfaction, a soft expansion in his belly and breath. An old soul who still hears and speaks the language of plants and trees, rivers, and stars.

Tea and warm porridge ready, he switches off the single light, feeling a sense of relief as the cottage returns to candlelight and shadows, as once again his eyes relax and widen. Again he sits upon the padded bench in the alcove of windows, a yellow throw pillow behind his back, round table beside him, and peers through the panes into darkness. The world seems darker now, though day will soon arrive in its painted, vivid glory, and once more things will regain their memory of color and shape, along with the illusion of separateness.

The various standing stones are etched against the shimmering backdrop of pewter sea, while the familiar shapes of the Dancers stand perpetually in their graceful poses. Come what may, the day begins in quiet appreciation of beauty and interconnectedness. A prayer for all beings.

Grace feels omnipresent.

In the hours of daylight ahead, whatever the weather that unfurls – cool and foggy, or warm and clear – the man will be pulled into the work that awaits, the tasks and trials of his day. The modern manmade world is noisy, demanding, and quarrelsome, but this dawn has been met with mindful intention, an open heart, and expansive breath. May such qualities persist, and be carried forward through the stream of waking hours.

For those who are paying attention, the holy is everywhere near... breathing quietly together in a shared inspiration.

In beauty, all is begun.

❧ ❧ ❧

The Cook and the Mango Tree: Ordinary Blessings
(July 2015)

I need to feel the earth under my bare feet.

Just a few hours ago, I was hurtling across the blue Pacific, returning home to Hawaii, my partner, and a houseful of guests. Honestly, I'm feeling more than a little tired and ungrounded.

Standing in the kitchen of our Kailua house, preparing dinner for the visitors who depart tonight on a red-eye flight, the compelling urge to be barefoot outside suddenly feels insistent. Never mind that my hands are thickly coated in an Indian-style yogurt marinade that I'm massaging into the segmented remains of some free-range chickens.

I feed people, it's what I do. Fresh, homemade fare that nourishes the *bodysoul.*

Despite my own long day of travel, on the way home from the Honolulu airport, we stopped at Whole Foods Market in Kailua where I wandered around and gathered some basics with which to make a meal for the six of us. Nothing elaborate, I'm too knackered for that, and being summer in Hawaii, where most houses don't have air conditioning, it's too damn hot and humid to even consider cooking anything that requires more than a few minutes on the stove.

I have decided to grill some Indian-style chicken and serve it atop a saffron rice pilaf, with a fresh green salad alongside. Once the yogurt sauce is slathered over the chicken pieces to soak up the flavors for a couple of hours, I can rest my tired bones until just before dinner. Ideally the saucy fowl would marinate overnight, but a few hours will have to suffice.

To a thick, Greek-style plain yogurt, I've added minced garlic, ginger, fresh lime juice, salt, chiles, cumin, cardamom, cloves and a kiss of cinnamon. The cumin and cardamom seeds I have both toasted lightly in a heavy skillet, and then crushed them using my *suribachi* – a Japanese mortar and pestle with ridges carved along the inside of the ceramic bowl for better traction and grinding.

Making incisions into the chicken pieces, I work the fragrant marinade into the flesh, thoroughly coating the segments on both sides, an aroma of spices rising with an exotic note, and set the lot to rest in the fridge until this evening.

I purchased two large, ripe, mottled green and red mangoes grown on the Big Island. These I will dice finely with some organic cucumber and cilantro, add a squeeze of lime, and spoon the juicy-sweet goodness atop the grilled chicken and saffron-infused rice.

The humidity makes me perspire, and I'm already missing the temperate coast of California. As I step from the house into the verdant and rustling landscape, a welcome breeze dances over me, wicking away a bit of the sticky heat. The cool of the stone *lanai* and then the soft grass beneath my bare soles feels very close to a sigh of relief.

The lush green, tropical world enfolding me offers a startling contrast to the parched brown of California in its drought-plagued summer. I know that in a few days I'll gradually adjust, but right now the island air feels oppressively hot and humid, and I'm sweating from every pore. The breeze is a godsend.

A floral *lei* of intoxicating tuberose is draped around my neck and shoulders, a welcome-home-to-the-islands gift from my beloved at the airport. The perfume of the white buds is heady and sweet, one of my favorite tropical scents – like the fragrant plumeria (frangipani) blossoms, it captures for me the essence of Hawaii.

Slowly I cross the lawn towards the venerable mango tree, the focal point at the edge of the ravine beyond, one of the special Standing Ones in my life that I am inordinately fond of. We are friends, this lovely old being and I, and I note immediately that the long, tongue-like leaves are bright, vivid green rather than dark. They seem to glow with new life, animated from within.

Several years ago, long before we moved to this house, the tree was heavily damaged in a storm, losing most of its upper, central trunk. Severely pruned so it might survive, according to the landlord, it has never born fruit since the trauma of the storm and being so harshly cut back.

When we arrived to live here two years ago, the thick brown trunk – a circumference equal to three or four men standing together – was tightly wrapped in a corset of non-functioning, old Christmas lights. I could almost hear the tree begging to be cut loose of the restrictive wires embedded in its rough bark, and on the second day of my residence, I marched out with a pair of wire cutters and freed it.

Looking at the mango tree now, admiring its shape and the way the wind dances through the thick foliage, it seems vibrant, healthy and happy. Someday soon it's going to bear fruit again, I think.

My senses widen to what surrounds – the scents, sounds, sights, and energetic feeling of the island – and I wiggle bare toes down into the thick green grass. After too many hours hurtling through the atmosphere in the belly of a great metal bird, how good is this tactile reconnection of sole, soul, and soil.

The frenzied jostle and chaos of airports, the buzzing electromagnetic energy and noise, the queues of people funneling through transportation security and boarding the plane, I find all of it tiresome. It is the most draining and tedious part of traveling.

Now with restorative earth under my feet, admiring the giant mango tree, listening to an island breeze as it dances *clackity clackity* in the swaying palm trees, and the *coo coo*-ing of little zebra doves, I feel my nervous system unwinding gently – slowing down, a gentle softening of belly and breath. It's a sense of coming home to myself after being uprooted and jangled about, barreling through a noisy, harried, technological world.

Gazing out across the wild jungle of the ravine, with a twinge of sadness I realize that this is the last time that I'll return to this gracious house. For a dozen reasons, including my ongoing presence in California, we've decided to let go of this lovely sanctuary.

The painted gypsy wagon rolls on again.

In the coming week, as this nomad has done so many times before, I will box up our belongings and get us moved to our next campsite. Given the heat and humidity, it's not a task I am looking forward to, but such is life.

Chop wood, carry water... pack boxes.

I feel a faint tingling in my feet and lower legs, the energy and negative ions of earth gently working subtle magic on my physiology, recalibrating me after the long travel. I know from experience that if I spend just half an hour barefoot outdoors, "earthing," I'll suffer little or no jet lag, and will effortlessly make the transition to my new locale.

The task of packing up the house looms large, and in my newly minted columnist role I have articles to write in the next days as well. It all feels slightly overwhelming at the moment, but I have been here before – too many times, really – and I know to take a couple of deep breaths and keep my feet on the ground.

One step at a time, River.

Savoring the cooling breeze, I briefly go over my list of kitchen tasks in my head, making sure that nothing else needs to be done right now. I want to rest for a bit beneath the fan of our bedroom, a little siesta before I rouse to get dinner on the table for the guests.

Truth be told, I'm feeling anything but social, but I will rise to the occasion and we will gather at our long rectangular table in the dining room with windows and doors ajar to the evening. Like a soft round of applause, the wind rustling the great thicket of bamboo just outside will serve as a backdrop to our animated conversation, and we will feast on a good, simple and fresh meal.

How many times have I written about the grace of the table, how it rests at the center of our lives..?

I'm still admiring my friend the mango tree when I note that high in its branches hangs a single, large green orb, and a childish grin of delight breaks across my face.

How wonderful. Despite the setbacks, losses and challenges, life goes on. *It bears fruit*, no less.

I often say in these posts that blessed are the ones who find beauty and amazement in the most ordinary, familiar things, we who recognize them as the treasures of life. Friend, here's hoping that whether it be the grace of the table, the fresh ingredients we have gathered, the sensation of being barefoot on the earth, a ripening mango, the wind in the trees, the light in our lover's smile – anything, really – that we take a moment to pause and appreciate.

Savor it... and blessed be.

A Recipe: Indian-style Chicken
Serves 4–6

Ingredients:

1 free-range, organic chicken, cut into pieces
250g (1 cup) plain yogurt
2 tablespoons fresh lemon juice
2 tablespoons minced garlic
2 tablespoons grated fresh ginger
1 ½ tablespoon ground cumin
2 teaspoons ground coriander
½ - 1 teaspoon cayenne pepper
½ teaspoon ground cardamom
¼ teaspoon ground cloves
¼ teaspoon freshly ground black pepper
1 teaspoon sea salt

For garnishing:

fresh ripe mango, diced
1 small cucumber, peeled and diced
fresh cilantro (fresh coriander)
juice of half a lime

Method:

Prick the chicken pieces all over with a fork and, using a sharp knife, cut slashes in the flesh. Place the chicken in a wide, shallow dish and sprinkle both sides with some sea salt.

To make the marinade: in a glass or ceramic bowl, combine the yogurt, lemon juice, garlic, ginger, cumin, ground coriander, cayenne pepper, cardamom, cloves, black pepper and salt. (I prefer to toast whole cumin and coriander seeds, along with black cardamom, and then grind them.) Stir until well mixed, then pour the mixture over the chicken and work it into the flesh, turning the chicken several times. Cover and marinate in the refrigerator, preferably for 8 hours or overnight. Remove the chicken from the fridge at least 30 minutes before cooking.

The chicken may be grilled or roasted. A gas-fired grill is convenient and works well. Preheat the grill on high for ten minutes or longer, lower it to medium heat, and place the chicken pieces on the oiled grate (which helps prevent sticking). Lower the heat and cook, turning occasionally, knowing that bone-in pieces require longer than boneless ones. Near the end of cooking, spoon additional marinade over the top and allow to cook through.

If using a charcoal grill, prepare the fire for direct-heat cooking, and position the grill rack 5 inches from the fire. Allow the coals to burn until white ash covers them and the heat is moderate. Remove the chicken from the marinade, pressing lightly to extract excess marinade, and brush with oil. Place the chicken pieces on a well-oiled rack and grill, covered, with the vents open, turning 3 – 4 times, until the juices run clear when a piece is pierced near the bone with a knife, 35 – 40 minutes.

If roasting the chicken, preheat an oven to 450°F (230°C). Place the chicken in a roasting pan and cook, turning once, until the juices run clear when a piece is pierced near the bone with a knife, 25–30 minutes.

While the chicken cooks, finely dice the mango, then peel and dice the cucumber, and combine them with the chopped cilantro/fresh coriander in a small bowl. Add a good squeeze of lime. When the chicken has cooked, spoon the mixture on top.

Serve with rice, or as desired.

◆ ◆ ◆

Reconsidering Success: Shadows and Light
(September 2016)

In the darkened womb of the round, earthen chamber, its center altar lit by a lone white taper candle, I sat quietly on my mat. Outside, unseen by me but their energy omnipresent, the tall trees stood sentinel, whispering stories and songs of the ages at the edge of a restless, dark sea.

I had driven north to the coastal redwoods to attend a healing retreat—an ayahuasca ceremony—and now I rested in the great kiva, a thirty-foot wide ceremonial room dug into the earth, with more than a dozen other people sitting quietly. As part of preparing for the event, we had been asked to carefully consider our intentions, and among several key pieces that I wished to examine on this journey were my notions of success and failure.

The bare dirt walls encircling us were studded with small alcoves, each niche holding a candle, at least fifty in all. Other than a round skylight twenty feet above, an eye of violet sky, already sparkling with a few diamonds of stars, the candles provided the only illumination in the great room. Sitting upright, legs crossed, I silently scanned the circle of unfamiliar faces, perceiving some of them as burdened with the weight of sorrows, others looking peaceful and joyous; each on his or her own quest for healing.

Upon the central altar I had placed a copy of my first book, *The Bones and Breath*, along with a few other items that represented facets of my life's journey, both as *healer* and one who seeks his own transformation: a bear claw necklace from a Native American medicine man, a Maori carved whalebone pendant, a ceremonial fan made of brightly-hued feathers, and my custom-made, blue opal and diamond wedding band. Seated in the East of the wheel – direction of new beginnings, dawn, insight and inspiration, vision, spirit – I gently regarded the book's familiar cover from ten feet away, considering it as a tangible record of my wandering path these past years, of both personal and transpersonal growth, and as an intimate offering to the Larger Story.

In my mind's eye, I recalled the long struggle to bring that book to the light of day – polishing and editing various drafts, cutting entire chapters and adding new ones, ever wrestling with my ongoing desire to craft a thing of beauty while feeling that I always fell short – and the search for its publisher. Each phase felt distinctly like climbing a mountain, exhausting and discouraging, the taste of dust and sweat in my mouth, with only dogged determination to spur me on.

In the flickering light and smoky air that smelled thickly of sage, as the white-haired, Huichol-trained shaman to my left offered a long prayer and another song to the invisible powers, I considered my disappointment – anguish, even – that after publication the book had received essentially no press or reviews, and thus remained languishing in quiet obscurity, selling only one or two copies a week, sometimes not even that.

What does it mean to be a success? A failure...?

Marlena de Blasi, internationally best-selling author of *A Thousand Days in Venice* and *A Thousand Days in Tuscany*, a new friend, recently wrote to me regarding this very concept as I anguished over the rough draft of my latest manuscript I had shared with her.

> "Letting go of notions of success – what is that? – as well as failure, which I understand even less, is fundamental. When either loom, they drive us. Pummel us, and, I think, invite us to act in some way falsely. As though someone is watching, judging."

I know she is correct, for I have been beaten down by my own notions of failure since the book emerged into the world almost two years ago.

My larger, overlighting intention for the healing retreat was to die to the old, limiting notions, patterns, and habits that no longer served my highest good, like anger and self-loathing. The same for doubt, criticism, and harsh judgment. Add "fear of my own power" to the list, too. In seeking the deeper realms of transformation, I knew that I needed to consider those ways in which my own beliefs and unconsciously chosen restraints held me back.

If we are paying attention, Nature models infinite lessons, teaching us at every turn, and I've written elsewhere that I've learned more from her than I ever learned in school. In certain respects, our personal growth resembles rings of a tree; we become larger and more expansive than younger versions of ourselves, still containing those smaller circumferences yet also exceeding them. At each stage, we may or may not even acknowledge that we are growing, and we don't yet perceive the wider, larger Self and worldview that we will later embody. We might detect the earlier phases and versions passed through and outgrown, but not yet the larger ones to come. Similarly, *we cannot actually grasp the full reality of those with a wider worldview than our own.*

Reality is *so* much bigger than the material world and human culture that we perceive; larger even than the miraculous world we glean through expansive senses, an open heart, and active imagination. Far more mysterious, too.

I have received beautiful letters, affirmations, and thank you's from unknown readers around the globe in response to my work, both *The Bones and Breath* and the Soul Artist Journal. Surely that alone is *success.* And I remind myself that an offering has been made – *continues* to be made through my ongoing efforts and work – and the Universe will decide how and when it chooses to accept such overtures. Our job is not to compare ourselves to others or decide at what point we have "arrived" or failed, but simply to create and give ourselves away, turning our energies into a stream of ongoing acts of sacred reciprocity.

Repeatedly I have said that one of the hallmarks of a Soul Artist is the continued letting go of smaller versions of self, those chosen limitations (wounds, roles, doubts, etcetera) we cling to, while seeking to expand into a larger, more authentic being guided by soul rather than ego. Such transformation is not easy. It isn't for the feint of heart. Growth requires bumping into, even stumbling around, lost in those dark, thorny, and painful places of the psyche in order to finally heal them. Indeed, our shadows persist *until* we meet them, and the soul's path is always an Underworld journey during which we may be totally dismembered before we reemerge to the daylight realms.

How does one describe the moment when he/she finally heals something and lets it go? Or a journey of death and rebirth? Words mostly fail.

In the candlelit chamber in a circle of brave souls, listening to the heartbeat of a drum and the old shaman's cracked voice singing his "medicine songs," I felt myself approaching some liminal threshold, my worldview expanding. Those older, smaller notions of self and identity labeled "writer" and "author," I was shedding them, leaving them on the earthen floor like a translucent snake skin. Or clothes that I've outgrown, realizing for the first time how threadbare they actually were. And my notions of success and failure, with an exhale of thanks, these I gave to the dancing flame on the altar and the spirits hovering near, offering them as sacrifice.

Holy, holy.

In my own journey as a healer, I've learned this: under all our layers of "stuff" and shadows, we really are *light*. But we don't find that illumination by seeking transcendence, we uncover it by venturing into the shadows.

Friend, here's hoping that on your own path of healing and transformation, whatever that looks like and wherever it leads – from a self-help book to a therapist's couch, a wilderness vision quest or shaman's fireside circle, traveling to a foreign country or starting a new chapter of life, or perhaps simply the crucible of intimate relationship and finding what is yours to offer the more-than-human world – that you will slough off the old, hardened layers, those limitations that no longer serve your progress. And in that disrobing, whether it be rough or gentle, may you emerge as something much lighter, bolder, graceful and free, though it may feel tender and awkward at first.

Remember, beneath all those shadows and weight, you are a radiant, beautiful soul, and the world awaits what *you* will bring.

❧ ❧ ❧

Little Messengers of Mystery: The Blue Bird
(March 2014)

I've been feeding the birds lately.

Sitting on the deck in lovely Carmel Valley, where I've been once again for a writing and work retreat, I'm falling back in love with the little garden birds that live here. My personal favorites are the iridescent, acrobatic hummingbirds – one just zoomed loudly by me as I wrote those words – but I also delight in the various sparrows and small, perching ones who alight on the deck railing. Or the outdoor bistro table and chairs. This being coastal California, there is plenty of food for them about but I've started placing seeds and grains on the deck as an enticement to draw them nearer to me.

Years ago in Taos, New Mexico, I used to feed the little winged ones each morning, scattering handfuls of golden millet on the brick patio. It didn't take long for the house sparrows, dark-headed juncos, and others to figure out that I was responsible for the sudden abundance, and they would line up outside on the adobe wall, twittering and waiting for me to emerge each morning to provide their winter breakfast. Offering made, I would sit inside in the warmth of my beloved jewel-box casita with a cup of good tea and watch their antics through the window, amused by the petty dramas that erupted.

Who needs television when you have birds to watch? Far more entertaining.

This morning, as I trailed a long, yellow-beaded ribbon of organic millet along the deck railing, I noted the dark-headed Oregon junco perched on the trellis nearby watching me. While it brought back recollections of New Mexico, for some reason it also triggered the memory of a curious incident whilst living in England, at our brick cottage in the green countryside of West Sussex.

My writing room was upstairs on the top floor beneath a steeply gabled roof, accessed by a nearly vertical narrow set of wooden stairs; a "loft" the Brits would term that upper space, though Americans would more likely call it a refurbished attic. I called my upper floor sanctuary "the Sky Kiva," and it had a large skylight in the sloping ceiling through which I would watch the nearly endless rain, and a narrow window in the far wall. Directly level with my eyes, beyond the leaded panes of glass, the upper branches of a rowan tree fanned wide, its delicate limbs crusted with a pale, sage-colored lichen. Barren of leaves in the wintertime, the thicket of silvery green, wooden fingers was often bejeweled with little black and white-banded birds called Coal Tits. Sometimes a red-breasted woodpecker would join the party, dressed in stylish ebony and ivory stripes and spots, with a vivid cranberry tail and breast. Such a strapping fellow, what a treat to be so close to him!

Often, too, there would be a couple of Blue Tits, adorable little birds sporting a soft yellow underbelly, with pale blue and white hooded heads. Precious, they are. As I sat at my hobbit-sized writer's desk, I would often pause while working on the book manuscript, delighted in their twittering capers, watching them clinging upside down to the branches just a few feet away or even on the window hinges. Blue Tits – what a name! – were my favorite miniature birds in England (though owls are my personal "totem" and guide, along with hummingbirds). Ever since our arrival at the cottage, even before setting up my sanctuary in the loft, when seated and writing at our large rectangular dining table, I smilingly observed those animated, colorful ones on the grey stone terrace. The Blue Tits seem less inclined than others to alight on the ground for the birdseed that I would scatter about. Gourmands, no doubt.

One morning in early December, I made my way downstairs to make tea and breakfast, carrying the laundry basket full of clothes for washing. In the kitchen, I opened the door to the small utility room and heard a tumult of scratching and rustling. I froze, thinking for a moment that a rat or mouse had somehow found its way inside. Damn. Just then I heard distressed chirping, a commotion that seemed to be coming from the window above the sink. Was it birds outside? I craned my neck and listened carefully from around the corner. No, it was definitely inside the house. I set down the basket of clothes and stepped quietly into the utility room, peering around the small, Euro-sized fridge to see the window.

There, inside the glass, peeping loudly and hurtling itself against the clear square panes was a Blue Tit. His or her mate was on the other side of the glass outside, peeping loudly in return, each trying to get to the other but confounded by the invisible barrier between them. I stood for a minute in utter astonishment. *How on earth did this little one get inside?*

The window in the utility room was perpetually locked shut, we had no key, and thus I could not simply open it to set the captive free. Baffled by the mysterious situation, I thought for a moment and then walked to the front door and opened it to the cold morning, giving myself an unobstructed path to escort the bird outdoors. Then I went back to the kitchen where I paused, filling my entire being with love and the spirit of gentleness. Calmly, I stepped into the laundry space and began moving things from the windowsill – liter-sized green glass bottles of sparkling water, cans of San Pellegrino *limonata*, etcetera – which the visitor was crashing into.

Cans and bottles removed, I slowly moved my hands toward the glass – fanned out and forming sort of a loose cage – and scooped the Blue Tit into cupped palms, which then I curled around him protectively. My own heart fluttering like rapid wingbeats, I stood there for a moment holding the petite one, and then walked to the living room. I adored the feel of tiny-taloned feet and the thrum of blue wings between my hands. Even when he pecked me with his beak, it didn't hurt but just seemed part of the sweetly curious experience.

Dressed for work in suit and tie, my partner descended the stairs just as I was going out the front door.

"I have a Blue Tit in my hands!" I gushed with childish excitement my brown eyes wide in delight.

As I reached the entryway, sensing freedom, the miniature blue and yellow bolt exploded from my hands, zooming off into the tall, conical cypress that stood beside the fish pond on the edge of the terrace. I walked through the open door, following the bird's meteoric flight with my eyes and stood outside, embraced by the chilly air of the cloudy morning with the flat grey stones icy cold under my bare feet.

The visitor zoomed off from the cypress, joined immediately by its mate, and I stepped back inside the warmth of the house. Still trembling with delight, entering the utility room again, as I began returning bottles and cans to the windowsill, I found a small, blue grey feather next to the glass. I smiled. I collect special feathers when I find them, and later I placed the miniature gift next to various others on the windowsill of the Sky Kiva.

Buzzing from the experience, utterly puzzled by the event, I stood in the kitchen and brewed my winter ritual of spicy, warming chai. Deciding not to make my usual warm porridge, instead I pulled from a cupboard the box of Rude Health organic muesli, noting with a grin the irony that it was called Early Bird.

The entire mystery of the episode, catching the Blue Tit in my bare hands, thrilled me. To this day, the logical aspect of my mind doesn't comprehend how the bird got inside the utility room, for there is no easy explanation – other than it simply being another clever agent of Mystery. Perhaps the little visitor was simply part of the not-so-subtle conspiracy of curious events designed to help me awaken from ordinary reality. Truthfully, as I roamed on foot through the woods, dells, and fields of that Old World landscape, my heart open wide to the 'other-than-human' world that surrounded me, I experienced a myriad of strange events and special encounters. Further tales for another time, perhaps.

Magic happens, you know, but to notice it one usually has to be paying attention. And when it does appear, our agnostically inclined minds are quick to dismiss it away.

Thinking about the encounter, I guess I should be immensely glad it was a Blue Tit in the laundry room and not, say, an owl. I would have shit my pants if I'd walked in and found a barn owl banging against the glass.

Seated on the deck in Carmel Valley and writing this post, preparing to return to Hawaii tomorrow, as I feed the little local birds I feel a sweet sense of connection with this place. I've spent many hours in these past couple weeks quietly walking the land – barefoot, generally – or parked outside, writing, absorbing the sights and sounds and *feel* of my surroundings through expansive senses. Listening. Paying attention. Simply *being* with what surrounds. Offering heart-centered appreciation, sometimes silent and other times spoken aloud.

A mark of Soul Artists is that they cultivate a personal relationship with the place where they dwell. There are countless ways to do this, of course, but it might include eating locally grown food, supporting local businesses and artists, dilating senses and heart to the energy and details around us, building hometown community, volunteering, tending a garden, walking the land (or neighborhood), and feeding the wild ones. In its own way, each of such actions underscores and strengthens our interconnectedness, especially when done with awareness. *Everything is relationship.*

As I repeatedly say and write, whenever we offer the gift of our attention – when we slow down, become mindful, see, sense, and feel – we draw closer into conscious relating, both with human and *other*. In that paying attention, hearts open with a gentle wonder or even awe. Soul Artists tend to see and engage the world differently than others do, and they often encounter the simple everyday magic that others miss.

Gentle reader, here is hoping that you find ways to draw closer into relationship with where you reside, appreciating beauty wherever you find it. Much is given to us yet we tend to offer little in return. Perhaps what we give could be something as simple as feeding the birds or wild ones.

The colorful, clever "agents of mystery and seduction" are everywhere, trying to wake us up from humanity's modern trance. So if you meet a curious little bird in your laundry room or encounter some other unexplainable event, consider that perhaps the Larger Story is trying to signal your attention, to expand your notions of possibility.

Blessed be.

❧ ❧ ❧

Honey Bees and Inspiration
(August 2012)

Acloudy afternoon. I am seated at the large, rectangular dining table with a notebook, gazing distractedly upon the lush green tapestry of foliage that surrounds our "tree house" here on the slopes of Haleakalā. The doors are open to the *lanai*, my two English Whippets are passed out on the floor for their seventh nap of the day, and from somewhere out in the distance, the whining drone of a chainsaw cuts the silence repeatedly. As I "zone out" and stare through the large windows, every few seconds a small, darting, golden missile flies across the view. My honey bees are out and about, zooming forth on their endless missions to gather pollen and nectar from the mountain or returning home with their cache to the white box that houses their colony.

I was hoping to work the bees today – opening up the hive, removing frames and looking for the queen, checking the state of the brood and cells of honey – but the sun isn't out. Though it is not raining, it isn't ideal bee weather. No matter the outside climate, these busy little, winged alchemists of nature keep the inside of their home at a very constant temperature with the fanning of their wings. If the roof is lifted off, they're in a much better mood about the situation if the day is sunny and warm, no cool breeze suddenly blasting into their cozy space. It's understandable, really; if I was seated comfortably in my living room, reading a book or working on a project, and someone suddenly opened the front door (or took the entire roof off) and left it open so that cold air was pouring in, I'd be grouchy too.

Due to the tall trees that completely surround this house and because of where the hive is situated, there is only a certain portion of the day that the colony receives full sun; roughly a four-hour period that is optimal for "working" the bees. Alas, that window was veiled with clouds today. Perhaps tomorrow... though I've been saying that each day for a week now, but the midday weather has not cooperated with my human agenda as a bee steward.

This being a starter colony with a young queen, I like to check on the state of things fairly often (but not so often that I'm bothering them), about once a week, just to make sure that everything is buzzing along nicely. Mostly, my concern is that the golden queen (Lucinda, I've named her) is laying well and that there is *brood* (unborn bees) in all the key stages of development. As a small hive, the colony's main objective at this point is increasing its size rather than simply building up reserves of honey. One of the lovely benefits of tending bees in Hawaii is that they don't have to survive a cold winter; a wealth of plants are always in bloom and pollen is abundant, thus the bees make honey year round.

The creation of honey is a staggeringly labor-intensive process. As outlined in the award-winning travel narrative, *Honey and Dust*, by Piers Moore Ede:

> *"Considering that the average bee will produce only about 1½ teaspoons of honey in its lifetime, it takes about 5,300 bees to gather enough nectar to make a pound of honey. One jar of honey is also the result of about 80,000 trips between flower and hive, the result of about 55,000 miles of flight, and the nectar from about 2 million flowers."*

Not only does this insight put the actual value of honey into perspective (more valuable than gold, I say), the endless work of these amazing creatures to produce a relatively small output gives me a sense of encouragement. Inspiration. There have been countless times – particularly recently in editing my book manuscript – when I felt that my daily efforts didn't add up to much.

And yet I haven't worked nearly so hard (nor so constantly) as an average honeybee in a day. I can only trust that by the end of my lifetime, I will have written and accumulated enough words and pages to equal that precious teaspoon and a half of honey from a worker bee. If I am very lucky, I too will have transformed some of nature's nectar into a bit of golden sweetness to offer the world through words, insight, and authentic action.

I often sit in a folding beach chair that I place two or three feet from the white bee box hive; doing a bit of writing in a notebook, enfolded by the sonic hum, and observing the activity as "the girls" come and go. Being around the bees is always a sort of meditation for me and I learn a great deal from simply observing them. They will each move through and serve many roles within the colony during their lifetime – nurse bee, builder, guard, gatherer – and each one of them is completely attuned to purpose and totally dedicated to the welfare and survival of the colony. In our modern world, this is something that we've lost; very few of us have any tangible sense of *meaning*, what our authentic roles or gifts might be, or how those talents might serve our community at large. Little of our work in the world seems meaningful, which makes it all the more likely to feel that our efforts and actions don't count overly much.

Even if we have found a project or purpose that offers a soulful framework to build our days upon, there will still be times when the journey is difficult and uphill, where it seems that we're not accomplishing much, or that we're simply spinning our wheels. Though it has largely become the measure of our days, *productivity* isn't the key value of a life well-lived. Yes, creating and offering something of merit certainly adds to our sense of worth, but there is also tremendous value in surrendering to the mysterious currents that pull us in unexpected directions, along with simply learning to enjoy life; not through entertainment or distraction, but through the pleasure of our open senses and the vessel of the *bodysoul*.

The bees inspire me to keep working and they simultaneously offer a bit of solace that my modest efforts may still add up to something worthwhile. Life is always a dance between *doing* and *being* (or "bee-ing," perhaps). Some days I'm better at the *doing* aspect and some days I'm better at *being*; occasionally I strike the elusive balance between the two, and I find myself in perfect alignment, a sense of openness, vitality, and flow in body and breath. I treasure those days... they are surely part of the priceless gift of being human.

May your day unfold with unexpected blessings and inspiration, gentle reader. Too, may you find the work that brings you a sense of meaning, connection and delight – your Eros and passion – while savoring and celebrating the simple existence of simply *being*.

❧ ❧ ❧

Au revoir, Roberta

(October 2012)

Sitting with my ritual cup of morning tea, I opened my email and scanned down the Inbox. Noting the address of Galerie Urubamba and hoping it to be a response to the note I sent to a woman in France a day earlier, I eagerly clicked it open. It took a moment for my brain to connect the dots and the words to sink in. The reply was not from the person to whom I'd written but from her daughter, sharing the news that her mother had passed from the world a few months previous.

The shock was unexpected and so too the tears welling up in my brown eyes. I reread the email carefully once more, transported back to Paris and her large Left Bank flat where I had lived, now taking in the details of her last days. Abandoning my breakfast tea, I stood up and walked outside onto the *lanai*, where I drank in the morning sunshine amid the whispering trees as hot, salty tears rolled down. In a stream of Parisian memories, my heart cracked open wide.

Several years had passed since my last contact with Roberta. She was the fiery, brilliant, outrageously opinionated and obstinate woman with whom I resided while I attended Le Cordon Bleu. An American by birth, she moved to Paris more than forty years ago with her two young daughters (one adopted, one biological), and became an ex-pat determined to stay. After a few diversions, she ended up creating a business importing Native American art from both North and South America, establishing a boutique gallery just a stone's throw from the Seine. A lifelong friend of my deceased mother, repeatedly she had invited me to stay with her, to come and experience France, and thus expand my limited horizons.

In my thirties, while living on the Big Island of Hawai'i, I made a career shift from the healing arts and decided to attend culinary school. I had little interest in returning to the mainland and being away from my partner, but the opportunity of France – where food is akin to religion – and lodging in the Latin Quarter, well, that was a different opportunity altogether. I accepted Roberta's longstanding invitation, wired an outrageous sum of money to Le Cordon Bleu, and enrolled at the world famous school to pursue a Grand Diplôme in *cuisine et patisserie*.

Roberta possessed a rare intellect, a hot temper, fiercely held opinions, and was critical to a fault. She was generous and punitive, both. Each evening when I returned from school bearing the day's creation(s), she would enthusiastically devour whatever I had prepared while offering a no-holds barred critique. Mind you, I'd already gone through an evaluation by *chef* at the end of class, but this woman was a tougher critic than any of my instructors.

"This *pot au feu* is all wrong!" she would decry, gobbling down every bite.

"I can't believe they are teaching you to make it this way. It's wrong."

"These are the wrong apples for this *tarte aux pommes*!"

And so it went. A critical evaluation each day at school in *cuisine* or *patisserie* (or both), and another each evening at the dinner table. "Wrong" was a well-used word in her household. Very occasionally, perhaps in conjunction with a planetary alignment or rare astrological event, there was praise.

"These *madeleines* are perfect! You must teach me to make them."

In a simple, non-fussy way, she was an accomplished cook in her own right. At the twice weekly market at Place Maubert, a few streets away from her flat, she was a force to be reckoned with. Ferocious as she was charming, she elbowed her way in to get the best peach – or whatever her sights were set upon – among all the other pushy French housewives while arguing a point, haggling on price, or loudly swapping recipes with the vendor. She maneuvered her tall, stainless steel, two-wheeled market basket like a sports car driver, packing it to capacity in the most efficient manner. Victorious with our groceries, we would then sit at the corner café and enjoy *un grand café crème* – "pas trop chaud" ("not too hot"), always her brusque insistence to the waiter – as we watched the market activities before heading back to her flat, where we would stuff the small, Euro fridge totally full.

A self-proclaimed *gourmande*, she took it as her personal mission to initiate me into the vast world of French cheese.

"Americans know *nothing* about cheese!" she snorted.

It was delicious, stinky, wonderful, and sometimes overwhelming. To this day, I cannot even contemplate Camembert without remembering one morning when, rushing out the door to school, Roberta accosted me in the hallway to chastise me severely with an angry look in her eye.

"You have done a terrible thing!" she barked.

I stared at her, not comprehending, silently running through the list of terrible things I had done since the previous night. Idiot that I was, I had placed the perfectly ripe Camembert in the cheese box in the fridge (where all the cheese was kept, silly me). Apparently, I was supposed to place it in the vented, enclosed windowsill box beneath the kitchen window.

"You have ruined it! It's inedible now. Might as well eat rubber. What a waste! You owe me a replacement."

She stormed off to her bedroom and I trudged off to another day of *chou vert* in the classroom (I swear that eighty-percent of what we cooked in the second term of cuisine was cabbage).

Despite my mistakes, my year of *fromage* and the nightly cheese course was one of extraordinary discoveries and good taste. Even now, at the year end holidays I still go giddy and weak in the knees over the thought of dipping into a ripe, runny, Vacherin Mont D'Or in its round spruce box (not that I would ever be able to lay hands on such a treasure in Hawaii).

Thirty-odd years prior, with her two little girls she had moved into a condemned flat without any heat on Rue du Sommerard in the Latin Quarter, a few doors down from the Musée de Cluny (the museum of medieval art, built atop ancient Roman baths). Over the years, she had renovated the apartment totally and, thanks to Parisian rent control, paid a pittance for what was now a grand, three bedroom, three bathroom, palatial suite with high ceilings – including a dining room and salon – in a highly desirable area of Paris, equidistant between the Sorbonne and Notre Dame.

Frugal to the extreme, she kept the heat so low during the winter that I was constantly bundled up to keep from freezing. I soon purchased the heaviest goosedown comforter sold at La Samaritaine (one of the iconic French department stores) in order to stay warm at night in my pale yellow bedroom overlooking the central courtyard.

For Roberta, the world was black and white, with very few shades of grey. She was immensely fond of sweeping statements: "Everyone is bisexual, they just won't admit it." "No one in France drinks white wine."

"Don't speak to me in French," she commanded one evening when I asked her a question about local mushrooms. "Your accent is terrible and I cannot understand you." (This from a woman who spoke French with an accent, herself.) Thus I was sentenced to English in the household.

Like a werewolf subject to the phases of the moon, one never knew which side of Madame Roberta would emerge. After scolding or criticizing me for something (say, putting the vacuum cleaner away incorrectly or daring to answer the phone), out of the blue she would suddenly smile, "*Allez, mon cher*, get your scarf. I want to take you somewhere."

Then she would lead me on some special walk, strolling arm in arm along narrow cobblestone streets, showing me a hidden aspect of the city or visiting a lovely park or secret garden. This paradox of a woman loved her adopted home with all her proud and fiery heart, and she was intent upon sharing the best secrets of Paris with me. Whether it was a remarkable stationery store with beautiful handmade papers (my favorite fountain pen, with which I have written every word of my book, came from there), or a special tea shop (I owe my fondness for Mariage Frères to her), an exceptional boulangerie or charming bistro, or a little shop selling antique brass pastry tools, the discoveries were countless. Most of them wonderful.

Larger than life, Madame R. could have been a character in a movie, except that she would certainly be perceived as merely a caricature rather than a real woman. She had traveled the world, survived dozens of hair-raising adventures, lived in the Amazon, studied with shamans, worked with Steinbeck as a young editor – she claimed that after he wrote *Travels with Charley*, he had asked her to ghost write for him – and spoke at least five languages fluently (English, French, Portuguese, Spanish, Czech).

She taught me the art of setting a French table, insisted I drink my coffee after dessert (French-style rather than American), and often held intimate dinner parties with fascinating guests – a Nobel laureate, a blind medical intuitive, a former resistance fighter and arms smuggler – where intellectual conversation and animated discussions flew round the table so fast that my rudimentary French was utterly useless and lost.

"I don't have time to translate for you," she exclaimed one evening in the midst of a flurry of debate, throwing up her hands in despair. "Just listen and *understand!*"

Right. Got it. *Bien sûr.*

Along with *Non* ("no"), her favorite French word was the command imperative of "listen" – *Écoute!*

In the closet of the bedroom where I stayed, she had a large, framed photo of the revolutionary Che Guevara. When one day I asked her who it was, she exploded into a stupendous rage.

"Americans are so stupid and fucking ignorant! You should be ashamed! Did you learn nothing in school?!?"

This led into a long, political diatribe from her that left my head spinning, and I resolved to ask no more questions. Ever.

Our time together was transforming and challenging, both. She instilled in me an abiding love of most things French (despite my apparently poor ability at the language), yet perhaps the greatest gift that she gave me was related to her role as an adoptive mother.

During my time in France, I was very ill with severe blood sugar issues and I spent too many hours at the American Hospital across town, undergoing tests to determine what might be wrong. Was I diabetic? Adopted at birth, I had no medical history to draw upon. Roberta stood convinced of the importance of adoptees locating their birth parents, and had urged her own adopted daughter to do so. Despite my resistance, she laid several books upon my bed for me to read about adoptees who searched for their parents and the important psychological shifts that unfolded for them as a result.

"You will never be settled in life until you search for her."

Propelled by my medical crisis, once back home in America, I did search for my birth mother and eventually located her. An emotional roller coaster ensued but, in the end, finding and meeting Katherine was a profoundly healing journey. I have Roberta to thank for that.

By the time I left school and Paris, our relationship had deteriorated significantly. I couldn't wait to leave her flat with all its complicated rules and shifting moods and temperaments. It bothered me that she refused to say "thank you" for anything, whether it was an errand I had run or dinner I cooked. Not once did she utter the words. It was as if they pained her.

Upon my departure, she gifted me a wooden box of exquisite, genuine Laguiole cheese knives – a different shape blade for various types of cheese, *naturellement* – with the iconic Napoleonic bee emblem affixed to their handles.

"You'll be back," she said affectionately, her eyes soft with emotion.

"I'll always come back to visit," I replied, "I love Paris... and France."

She shook her head vehemently, one finger waving through the air in the all too familiar rebuttal. "Non! One day, you will be back to stay. I can tell." She hugged me goodbye, and then I turned and walked out her door with my suitcases and down the classic, spiral stairs of the old building.

I never saw her again.

We maintained email connections over the first couple of years, particularly during the search for my birth mother. She was terribly fond of mailing out blistering tirades against George W. Bush, an attempt to mobilize all Americans into action to take back their government. But eventually, we dropped the thread and silence ensued across the distance, oceans, and continents between us. Until this week, when I reached out to thank her for all that she had given me and being such a challenging but remarkable influence on my life.

Alas, I was too late. Cancer took her away, though she went to work at her beloved Galerie Urubamba until a week before her death. I can still see her marching down the sidewalk, shoulders hunched but head held high.

Roberta was a woman who lived with passion and conviction and I salute her. She pursued her dreams and ambitions with zeal and gusto, and I think she had a firm sense of her soul and what nourished it. Or didn't. As a single mother in a foreign country, she built a good life for herself and raised two worldly, competent daughters. Yet I suspect that given her true genius of intellect and firmly set opinions, she was profoundly lonely much of her life, for who could possibly compete or ever rise to her level? I feel compassion for her, along with deep gratitude that she was a vivid part of my journey.

In her own way, she was a Soul Artist. She cultivated pleasure, and in a very French manner lived for the delight of gathering at table with a well-crafted meal and good wine. Much of that she shared with me, sculpting with a forceful hand in curiously subtle ways. And I think both she and *la belle France* helped me realize that my sensitivities and appreciation for the sensual details of life were not an anomaly but something to be cultivated. Celebrated, even.

I've not yet returned to the Hexagon to live as she predicted – I landed for some years in England and then Spain, instead – but who knows. After residing abroad in various places, I'm inclined to say that the south of France (and the northeast of Spain) still holds a distinct allure to return and linger. Apart from the remarkable light and *joie de vivre,* I'd do it simply for the open-air markets, wine and cheese. Thanks to Roberta, I am ready with some lovely *couteaux à fromage.*

Au revoir et merci, ma cherie Roberta... je t'embrasse bien fort.

❧ ❧ ❧

Living at the Threshold between Worlds

(March 2013)

E vening has arrived early, padding stealthily down the mountain on soft cat's paws. Though it is only afternoon, daylight fades beneath pale ribbons of cloud that wrap around this little cottage and weave beguilingly through the surrounding green lattice of leafy trees. Looking out through broad windows and sliding glass doors, my verdant world is transformed under a spell of enchantment. It is as if ancestors and ghosts hover near, conversing with energies of earth, wood, air, and blossom, whispering to my soul in unheard voices.

As is so often the case in my life, I am at the threshold between worlds. For a few more weeks, we dwell on the upper slopes of windward Haleakalā, an elemental world of swirling weather and other-than-human forces. The old Hawaiians considered these cloud forests of the mountain to be the realm of spirits and voices in the trees, a place where humans should tread lightly. Living here for a year, I am not one to disagree.

On this quiet afternoon, I suspect the faerie mists will soon morph to a soft rain, ten-thousand invisible fingers tapping a steady cadence on the battered drum of the cabin roof.

Even the honey bees are hushed today, a collective reflection of the trailing mists and spirit forces that enfold us, and the bees' quietude reflects my own subdued inner mood. It is as if we all are humming in soft resonance together: mountain, mists, spirits, bees and man. Inseparable and interwoven in a gentle, delicate harmony or low chant from ages lost in memory. At the end of this week, the bees go to their new home as I begin preparations for our move to the busy island of O'ahu, a relocation that mandates leaving my dear "girls" behind on Maui. They will have an ideal location in a beautiful, healing garden of upper Olinda, but how I will miss these remarkable, golden-winged alchemists of nature.

I originally sat down to write about the honey bees but, as the foggy mists descended, found myself following a different, glimmering thread ... crossing a threshold between worlds.

An apt description of my life, I'd say. A preferred address, even considering my current dwelling (and previous ones), it's no surprise that I'd be drawn to the cloud forest of this Pacific mountain, the realm of spirits and elementals. At the edge of the forest or village is always where the shamans, witches, sages and healers dwelt. Madmen and undesirables, too. Often it's a fine and arbitrary line between such distinctions, one that is easily blurred.

Nowadays, it is mostly the Soul Artists – a beautifully diverse array of writers, poets, artists, guides, dreamers, mystics, "evolutionaries" and inspired souls – who choose to dwell at the edge. *Evolution always happens first at the fringes*, and the "edge dwellers" are the ones deeply attuned to the environment in which we breathe, grow, make love, and dream. We are the ones who realize that Earth is awake, a sentient being of which we are a creative part. We are the ones who choose to dive headfirst into the dark, mysterious waters of life as our souls expand in harmony, gratitude, wonder and awe. Whatever label we choose or are given, we will always be the ones tending the hearth at the threshold between worlds, whether literal or metaphorical.

Despite Western society's deeply ingrained agnostic impulse – a disbelief in invisibles – the living, mythic world is still as alive as it was in the time of Ulysses. Archetypes still emerge in every form and being. Intelligence, awareness and creativity are each inherent in any self-organizing system, while the line between living and non-living grows ever thinner. We have only to shift our perspective a bit, to open our senses and discover another realm of reality that slips in sideways at the peripheral edge of vision. Apart from night dreams, for most individuals it will nearly always be in "nature" or semi-wild places that we will discover that hidden dimension... waiting for us.

The threshold between worlds is the place where the dream and dreamer meet.

I admit, I'm hesitant about our impending move to Hawaii Kai near Honolulu, to a cookie-cutter house at the top of a manicured subdivision. Its location, design, and materials all feel mismatched to a wild, elemental soul. It's a somewhat odd and unlikely residence for someone who walks with a foot in two different worlds – an *edgewalker* – but I also trust in the curious process that has brought this about. Though the currents of fate remain unfathomable, I have faith in my bones regarding their mysterious guidance. And I sense too that just as with other times of sailing forward to new shores, the first place we alight is merely a landing spot.

From there, in a year or two, we will be drawn effortlessly to the "right" spot that is calling, waiting for us to come home and deepen into conscious relationship with house, sky, water, plants, soil... and soul. Yes, it will be just like that, for it always is for me. In the meantime, good things will happen in an unlikely house, and I will turn all my powers towards fashioning yet another Soul Artist sanctuary. We need not live on a mountainside to encounter the sacred and mythic, nor to live in a deliberate, heartfelt manner; we can greet the Holy each morning simply by stepping barefoot into our garden or yard. Or blessing the potted flowers on our doorstep. *Grow where you're planted.*

I have written elsewhere that "our senses are the threshold where we engage the world around us, where we stand in relation to the Sacred Other." Wherever we may be, whether in Seattle or Santiago, we are always at the threshold of awareness. When we begin to pay attention, to expand our breath and bodily awareness, we trigger a shift in perception. A doorway opens, inviting us into a deeper relationship with life, its overlapping realities and mythic dimensions. An everyday sort of magic occurs and enfolds us, an incantation wordlessly uttered *simply through the feat of paying attention.*

Here in a darkening cottage, the silvery cloud has swallowed us, as the mountain's breath and spirits are made visible once more. The familiar, whispering trees, the Standing Ones so close at hand, have withdrawn to become silent grey shapes in the shifting mists. A velvet silence lies thickly upon everything, inviting me to listen with my whole body, senses open wide, to the unheard song.

All of Creation is singing, and we are the only ones not paying attention.

At the threshold between worlds, I am listening, expansive in body and breath. Awake. Carrying a silk-wrapped bundle of luminous words and wild blessings to offer other pilgrims and wayfarers I meet, my vessel of bodysoul sails ever forward into deep blue waters of soul and mystery, a single word painted around the prow... or across my chest:

Believe.

❧ ❧ ❧

The Knowing Heart: An Organ of Perception
(October 2013)

The bees called me back to myself. To my heart, really.

One sleek English Whippet on a lead in each hand, I was somewhat groggily stumbling barefoot down our street this morning, taking "the boys" out for their morning walk. My head pounded with a trigger point headache (a chronic problem lodged deep in my suboccipital muscles), and I felt decidedly less than inspired to be out on doggy duty. About a dozen houses down from our current dwelling, both boys stopped simultaneously to do their business beneath a tall, "Rainbow Shower" tree, also known as a Java Cassia, adorned with countless cascading pink and yellow blossoms. Actually, it's my favorite tree on the entire street; something about its shape, shade, and gorgeous mantle of delicately-scented flowers.

Head throbbing and feeling decidedly out of sorts, feeling neither open nor expansive, as I stood aimlessly and waited for the dogs to poop, I heard the sound of honey bees buzzing nearby. As a former bee steward, the sounds of *apis mellifera* humming contentedly is a sort of melody that brings me instant comfort, triggering a harmonic resonance in my body. I looked up and noticed dozens of bees on the pink and golden flowers, all over the tree, delicately making love to the flowers and quietly buzzing with bliss.

I have often stopped beneath this particular tree, appreciating its shade on hot and humid days, appreciating its bio-energy field, admiring the pastel-hued raiment, and savoring its sweet smell. Yet I have never noticed more than a single bee or two on the blossoms. This morning they were everywhere, and it was their audible communion that brought me out of my head and back into my body and senses.

Wake up, River!

Observing the bees, I opened my heart and reached out with my own energy field to touch the rough trunk, the cool green leaves, the creamy blossoms – *feeling* each with a quiet, wordless sensing and appreciation.

The pain in my neck and head seemed to lessen as my focus shifted outwards.

On a recent retreat to the mainland, where I penned the new final chapter for my revised manuscript (now titled "The Bones and Breath: A Man's Guide to Eros, the Sacred Masculine and the Wild Soul"), I found myself writing about the heart as a primary organ of perception. Recent studies have revealed the heart as far more than merely a mechanical pump; greater than sixty percent of the heart is composed of neural cells, identical to those of the brain, and they work in the exact same way. In fact, the heart is actually a brain whose function is to interpret specific kinds of information – largely from the senses, primarily interpreted as *feeling*. A complex and incredibly rapid exchange exists between brain and heart; a two-way arrangement where impulses enter the heart and are transmitted to the brain, which then categorizes and sends this data back to the heart and rest of the body. (I won't get into the technical details here.)

The heart also produces the strongest electromagnetic field in the body, detectable several feet away, one that can *entrain* all the other body systems, including the brain. (It also affects other fields it comes in contact with, human and non-human.) When the brain entrains to the heart and becomes "coherent" with its field and rhythms, a cascade of positive physiological effects floods through the body (including a lowering of blood pressure, increased production of immunoglobulin A, along with a host of beneficial hormones and neurotransmitters). These scientific studies reveal what the artists, poets, lovers, shamans, and healers have always known: *the heart is our center of knowing.*

In our modern world, most of us have been conditioned to place our seat of identity and consciousness in the brain rather than the heart. In our daily lives, we function almost exclusively from a linear, analytical, rational mode, rather than a nonlinear, heart-centered, intuitive one. Men, especially.

Yet there is a direct response in the heart to what is presented to the senses.

A cellular response to our environment has guided humankind for millennia, a knowing in the heart through the direct perception of nature/environment. It is a wholistic mode of cognition – often wordless – that is distinctly different from the rational, linear, analytic mode that now dominates our world. As I wrote in a (somewhat lengthy) blog early this year, "Spirits of Cedar":

> *"In this form of sensing, of reaching out, there exists a moment when both beings experience something unique in the other. It's a feeling for which we have no word in our impoverished English language. The Athenians called such an awareness 'aisthesis': the experience of feeling the touch of life, of a particular kind of 'other-*

than-human' awareness upon us, in return. For the ancient Greeks, the organ of aisthesis was the heart, that part of us that is capable of feeling. It was understood that this exchange, this non-physical touch between humans and the non-human world, opens moments of perception and understanding, when insights flow into us that can arrive no other way."

Simply placing our awareness on a thing – feeling it through our senses, wordlessly – initiates this heart-centered, intuitive mode and begins the brain's entrainment to the heart's field (thus triggering the beneficial physiological response and a different state of being). Immediately there ensues a shift in respiration. Analytical thinking or verbal cognition breaks the entrainment and perpetuates the disharmony in rhythms between heart and brain.

Repeatedly in my writings, podcasts, coaching, and conversations, I emphasize the importance of opening through our senses and heart, that doing so is an *evolutionary* impulse of the soul and actually guides us on our personal journey. It's one of the primary ways that we become expansive – always the soul's mission – rather than contained and restricted in familiar patterns. Indeed, opening through our senses and heart is a primary Soul Skill (one of seven presented in my upcoming book).

Yet even for Soul Artists and those who endeavor to be "awake" in the world, there are times when we are less than open, not quite tuned-in. We're holed up in our heads rather than in our hearts. It's often in such moments when Nature or something in our environment – *poulet au pot* simmering on the stove, perhaps, or the contented buzz of honey bees – reaches out to touch us, to draw us gently back to the body and the present moment.

To what will we give the gift of our attention?

The world is a waiting lover, hoping to be seen, noticed, and appreciated. Adored. Marveled over. Not in a rational, analytical sort of manner but with an openhearted communion with the heart, knowing that what we perceive also perceives and touches us, in return.

Soul Artists understand, each in their own unique way, that the heart is an organ of perception. It guides them as they navigate their days and make their choices – often simply by the 'feel' of a thing or option – including the way it resonates in their body with a somatic response. On their own path of discovery and transformation, they endeavor to learn and employ – and trust – this heart-centered, non-linear mode of cognition.

Gentle reader, may you take moments throughout your day to simply stop what you're doing and shift into a heart-dominant mode that entrains the brain and body. Extend your awareness as if you were reaching out with the heart's field, and place your attention on something – tree, flower, rock, bird, cat, *objet d'art*, or person – and simply *feel* it. Wordlessly. Open your senses. Notice how your breath shifts and your entire physiology immediately recalibrates, also. The connection needn't be maintained for long.

The more you can do this throughout your day, you will begin to entrain the entire body to the heart's field and create coherence throughout bodymind – a positive state that yields dividends for well-being (and about which I'll tell you more next week).

Just for today, let your heart and senses be your guide, and experience the world as a poet or lover does... with *feeling*.

❧ ❧ ❧

Valentine's Day: Eros and Apples

(February 2016)

F ind Love in What You Read." What writer or book lover could resist such an invitation?

I clicked on the email from my publisher to open it. What a nice surprise to find my recent book, *The Bones and Breath*, among five titles promoted for a Valentine's Day sale. Personally I had never considered any connection between what I write and Valentine's, but how lovely to be featured alongside Rumi and Kahlil Gibran as a book that "explore[s] eros in profound ways..." (Thank you, White Cloud Press.)

To the ancient Greeks, Eros was the god of desire, the son of beautiful Aphrodite. A handsome and alluring divinity, Eros embodied the masculine aspect of love, a powerful deity in his own right. Sometimes regarded as a male fertility icon, the god of desire personified the energies of lust and intercourse, as well as beauty.

> *"The conquering Romans, in their adoption of the Greek pantheon, diminished mighty Eros into a pint-sized, chubby cherub. The handsome and arousing god devolved into the mischievous Cupid, hiding behind clouds to dart unsuspecting souls with his arrows of desire. In this infantile guise, mischievous but charming, Love fades as an elemental force of the universe, deteriorating from one that can join or break apart the fiery stars to something of mere ego romance.*
>
> *Further trivialized by our modern culture, Eros turned Cupid is now the stuff of candy valentines, hothouse-grown roses tied with satin ribbon, pop songs, and fluffy Hollywood movies."* (excerpted from *The Bones and Breath*)

I wrote most of *The Bones and Breath* whilst living in England, and on my trips into London's vibrant West End, I'd often stroll past the famous bronze Eros at Piccadilly Circus, a crowd of tourists clustered at the base of his pedestal. Personally, I appreciate that he was cast as an attractive male divinity rather than a little cherub.

Valentine's Day stirs mixed feelings in me. In my early twenties, my adoptive mother was buried on the day after, and for years the lovers' date remained clouded by the dark grief of her passing. I have long harbored a somewhat less-than-embracing view of Valentine's as mostly a commercial tryst when nearly everyone is scrambling to book a table at a nice restaurant, and buying their sweetheart some flowers and chocolate out of obligation (a sentiment I hold for most "greeting card holidays" like Mother's Day, Father's Day, etc.).

And then there's the shadow aspect: with its singular focus on romantic love, Valentine's Day can be a poignantly lonely time for those who are single or have lost their love (just as the year-end holidays can feel not-so-festive).

Similarly to how I feel about Thanksgiving, that rather than a single calendar day each year, *every day* ought to be one of giving thanks, I would much rather appreciate my beloved throughout the cyclical seasons with little tokens and gifts of affection. Flowers and presents given as a surprise often mean a great deal more, I think.

All that said, I appreciate Valentine's Day better than I used to. Twenty-five years have passed since my mom died, and twenty-four of those have been spent beside the blue-eyed Prince of Hearts, whom I eventually married beneath the flowering Wedding Tree in a Sussex country garden. Together we have roamed far as our painted gypsy caravan rolls ever onward (it occasionally sails across oceans), a pair of English Whippets onboard.

Though I seem to be getting sentimental in my age, you won't find us at a crowded, romantic restaurant tonight; I am happy to be at home and cooking something nicer than our ordinary weeknight dinner, with a favorite dessert alongside. (His request wasn't for chocolate but instead for a *galette aux pommes parfumée au thym*, one of my rustic tarts, the mildly sweet apples fragrant and savory with resinous thyme.)

Circling back to Eros, we don't have to be in love to celebrate or acknowledge this elemental energy of allurement. I would offer that eros *includes yet transcends* the sexual, that it is inseparable from the creative and spiritual. In a real sense, eros is the deep longing in the heart for connection to something larger, and a summons of the soul to offer something of beauty and value to the world.

For me, nature – our larger body – is always a significant part of my eros. At the risk of sounding overly dramatic, I simply cannot live without it. It draws me, comforts, heals, and connects me. Equally so with creativity, the blueprint of the soul. When our senses are expansive (as I'm so often advocating and writing about in this journal), beauty and the natural world reach into us while our innate creativity opens outward to meet that touch.

Eros is a sensual communion with the soul of the world.

This morning when I stepped from the cottage into the cool moist air, the resinous, almost lemony fragrance of Monterey cypress immediately greeted me. The scent lasted a mere few moments and then disappeared as my olfactory nerve quickly habituated to it. Simultaneously, I heard the low rumbling voice of the sea, half a mile distant, a sound that usually recedes amid the noise of the day as this little town comes awake with cars, twittering of birds, and general hubbub of life.

Both these sensory impressions were fleeting, just strong enough to register but easily ignored if one wasn't paying attention. Already my brain was working and ticking like a clock, thinking about what I needed to accomplish today, some inspiration on a chapter I am editing (read, gutting), and an idea or two for the Soul Artist Journal. Yet the soft caress of nature caught me and I stopped, inhaled a deep breath, and dropped my awareness down into my soles on the cool bricks covered thickly in yellow pollen from the pines.

Breath in my belly I stood with chin upturned, savoring the moment as it danced in my nostrils, ears, on my tongue. Feeling the coastal, morning air upon my skin. Two feet away, something glimmered at the edge of my peripheral vision, and my gaze was drawn by the first of the camellias opening in the morning sunlight, a small pink flower incandescent as if lit from within. Could anything be more stunningly perfect or elegant?

What grace to be alive and ensouled in this ordinary moment.

Beneath a soft blue sky my eyes swept the familiar patch of the front garden, noting little blush snowflakes upon the dirt, fallen petals of the ornamental plum blossoms that just last week I wrote of. How short-lived their delicate, perfumed beauty.

How much time do any of us have left? Or what measure of grace? And where is eros in our lives?

There isn't much time, really. Life is short and precious. *Love.* Love now. Don't wait for Valentine's Day. Or tomorrow. Go kiss your beloved tenderly on the nape of their neck and whisper to them that they are beautiful, how much you truly appreciate them. If you have no human beloved to kiss softly, then give the love to your dear pet instead. And if you have no animal companion, I say go outside and kneel to kiss the earth, praising the unsung goodness that sustains and nourishes us all.

Friend, wherever and whomever you are, here's hoping you will find, follow and celebrate *eros*. And whether it leads to the candlelit bedroom, an overgrown garden, a lonely shore or windy mountaintop, may you savor such communion with the sensuous soul of the world.

Blessed be.

§

This rustic tart seasoned with fragrant thyme is hardly traditional Valentine's Day fare, perhaps better suited to autumn when apples are at their peak, but I'm often an unconventional chap. And then there's the fact that love, like life, is savory as it is sweet. I prefer an unsweetened crust, and I usually make the filling with a minimal amount of sugar, which makes it delectable for breakfast should there be any left over. Rosemary offers an intriguing substitution for the thyme.

A Recipe: Galette aux pommes parfumée au thym
(Rustic Apple Tart with Thyme)
Serves 6–8

For the pastry:

200g (1½ cups) unbleached, organic, all-purpose flour (or finely ground spelt
    flour, but add more water)
Large pinch of sea salt
100g (7 tablespoons; 3 ½ oz) unsalted butter, chilled and cut into small pieces
50ml (4 tablespoons) chilled water
1 small egg

For the filling:

4–6 baking apples (preferably organic), cored, peeled, and cut into ¼-inch slices
50g (scant ¼ cup) sugar
1 tablespoon fresh thyme leaves
(or substitute fresh rosemary, finely chopped)

Method:

To make the pastry, place the flour and salt in a food processor and pulse to mix.
Add the butter and pulse about 10 times until the mixture resembles coarse
cornmeal. Add the water and process just until combined and crumbly. Turn the
dough out onto a lightly floured surface and gently press it into a cohesive ball.
Flatten into a disk, wrap in plastic cling film, and let rest in the fridge for at least
half an hour.

Whisk together the egg and 1 teaspoon of water to make an egg wash. Strip
the thyme leaves from their branches, chop if desired. Slice the apples (you can
squeeze a bit of lemon on them to keep from discoloring, but for a rustic tart this
isn't really necessary).

Preheat the oven to 425° F (220°C/gas 8).

Remove the pastry from the fridge and allow it to warm slightly. Lightly flour
a work surface and roll out the pastry to roughly a 14–inch (35.5 cm) circle.
Transfer it onto a baking sheet lined with parchment.

Layer the apple slices on the pastry, slightly overlapping them in an outer circle, then an inner one. Sprinkle with the sugar and the thyme. Bring the edges of the pastry up and over the slices, working your way around the edge by making soft pleats of the pastry. The apples won't be completely covered.

Brush the pastry with the egg wash. Place the galette to cook in the lower third of the oven until the pastry is golden and the apples are softened and their tips and edges have caramelized, about 45 minutes.

Let the tart cool to lukewarm or room temperature before serving. Share with someone you love.

❧ ❧ ❧

A Paris Encounter: Meeting de Blasi
(May 2015)

The probability was less than one in a million.

Or, as I like to say, a mysterious intersection of fate and destiny.

That I would happen to encounter one of my favorite authors sitting at a famous Left Bank café in Paris was improbable enough, yet a half dozen other factors that day led up to that moment and had any one of them not occurred, we would not have met. *Serendipitous* seems a weak word.

I arrived in Paris from the States on Wednesday, and apart from simply taking in the heart of this great city in springtime, I had two objectives for my brief visit: a return to the iconic, 19th-century cookware shop, E. Dehillerin, and a stop at a small Left Bank boutique shop, Huilerie J. LeBlanc, to procure another of their fabulous earthenware (*argile cuite*) bottles of artisanal Provençal olive oil, like the one I bought fifteen years ago when a student in Paris at Le Cordon Bleu.

Late on Thursday morning, I set out from our Right Bank hotel to walk to E. Dehillerin, which is not far from the Opera. It was roughly a mile each way, and by the time I returned to our hotel, I could feel my right foot beginning to ache. Our main plan for the day was to visit the Musée d'Orsay – once a grand railway station on the *rive gauche* (left riverbank), now home to Paris' second most famous museum and one of the finest Impressionist art collections in the world (though as we learned later, the iconic Monet water lilies have been moved to L'Orangerie). Shortly after lunch, my partner and I strolled through the Jardin de Tuileries, the long, tree-lined park that stretches along the Seine from the Musée du Louvre to the Champs Elysees, and crossed over the river to the museum. My foot hurt, but it wasn't terrible, and I was reveling in being back in dear Paris, soaking in my memories of living there years before.

Nearly a year ago I injured my right foot, and the subsequent plantarfascitis has continued to be a limiting story ever since. Long distance walking has been curtailed, and even with treatment and therapeutic insoles, my foot continues to trouble me if I ramble too far, stand too long, or dance.

With all the day's walking and standing, followed by the picturesque amble back across the river to our hotel, the ache in my foot had progressed to my knee and up to my right hip. I was limping slightly and in considerable discomfort, realizing that my ambulation for the day was finished. Indeed, I guessed that my mobility the next day might be somewhat compromised, as well.

Shortly after returning to the hotel room, we learned that the next day (Friday) was a bank holiday in France and, in typical fashion, nearly everything would be shut. With our train for Cannes departing on Saturday morning, suddenly there was little opportunity remaining to go to Huilerie J. LeBlanc, if it even still existed; similarly, several of the things we had planned to do on Friday now bowed out of the picture.

Looking up the shop on the Web, it seemed the shop was no longer was in business, but another little boutique on Rue Jacob sold the artisan oils from J. LeBlanc, and Robert, determined to help me acquire what I wanted, rang them up. Madame, in a mixture of English and French, informed us that she would be open until 7:00 but closed tomorrow. It was already 5:30.

"I'm not going back out," I shook my head. "I cannot walk any more today. The olive oil isn't that important... I'll get it next time I come back to Paris, whenever that may be." (Passing through to elsewhere, my previous two visits to the city had both fallen on a Sunday when the shops I wanted to visit were shut.)

We could take the Metro, my partner suggested, but I knew from my experience of living in Paris years ago that although the distance was short as a crow flies, crossing the river and then getting to St.-Germain-des-Prés from our current location involved three different metro lines. At peak commuter time, this hardly seemed appealing. Not only would we be squished like sardines into a packed and stuffy subway car, there would still be walking and stairs.

We could take a taxi, my mate offered, earnestly trying to get me the long awaited *huile d'olive* in its beautiful earthenware bottle. "That's crazy," I shook my head. "Traffic is at a standstill out there."

"You're not coming to Paris and not getting your oil," my beloved countered. "You've missed it on the past two trips."

In the end, I relented. We climbed into a taxi outside the hotel and then inched slowly along in gridlock, accompanied by French drivers agitatedly honking their horns, forcing their way in at intersections – though no one could move far or get ahead. "I'm sorry," said our Mediterranean driver, in flawless English, "Paris has a real problem."

When we finally managed to get across the river, still mired in traffic on Boulevard St. Germain, knowing that we were not far from the shop, I thanked the driver and we got out and walked – me, limping – the remaining blocks to Rue Jacob in the 6th *arrondissement*.

We found the little shop, tucked into a quaint courtyard with vines growing up the old building walls. Disappointingly, the elegantly rustic ceramic canisters that I had come for – their corks sealed with wax and looking decidedly Old World – had been discontinued in the large size, thus I had to content myself with *une petite. C'est la vie.*

Standing outside the shop I felt somewhat deflated. My foot and leg screamed silently.

"Let's get a taxi," offered my mate, each of us realizing that walking back to the hotel was simply out of the question. Cognizant that traffic remained snarled in every direction, car horns peppering the air as the bronze bells of St. Germain rang loudly for seven o'clock, I shook my head. "We'll spend another 20 euros just sitting in traffic."

I considered our options for a moment, then suggested we sit at a café for a while until *le embouteillage* (traffic jam) eased up, at which point we could hail a cab. Slowly we walked back to Boulevard St. Germain, where my partner pointed to a café on the corner and said, "That one looks nice."

I laughed aloud. The busy brasserie was Les Deux Magots, arguably the most iconic café on the Left Bank, made famous years ago as the haunt of the literary and intellectual elite of Paris – frequented by Simone de Beauvoir, Jean-Paul Sartre, and Ernest Hemingway, as well as Albert Camus, James Joyce, Picasso, and others. I explained a bit of its history.

"You'll pay a tourist price for the privilege of sitting there," I smiled wearily.

"I don't care. I want the experience... especially now that I know its relevance. Come on."

D'accord. I was too tired and achy to argue. I simply needed to sit. As we approached and scanned for an open table on the crowded sidewalk, a woman with bright red lips, expressive eyes, and hair the color of hot copper wires caught my attention. Seated at one of the front tables on the sidewalk, she wore fingerless lace gloves and a black lace cap, a wide-eyed expression on her face. A very distinctive looking woman – those large eyes and bright lips, the flaming hair – I recognized her from the jacket photos on her books.

"I think that's Marlena de Blasi," I said to my mate as we sat down at a small, just-vacated table. "And her husband, Fernando."

I could scarcely believe it. Marlena de Blasi, author of the bestselling memoirs *A Thousand Days in Venice*, and *A Thousand Days in Tuscany* (among other titles), sitting not a dozen feet away. A chef and writer who moved to Italy twenty-some years ago to marry a Venetian, de Blasi writes books that are gently steeped in delicious, rustic flavors and an attention to the small details of life. She has a penchant for the old fashioned, and authentic foods, for a life lived deliberately at a slower, more nourishing pace, and reading her works I have always imagined her as something of a kindred spirit.

Her engaging memoirs and stories often comforted me as an expat living abroad, offering a sense of being not quite so alone in a foreign world. It was she who first gave me the concept of a "survival ritual," those actions that center us in our sense of self and keep our little boat upright in challenging waters – like going to the farmers' market, or cooking a comforting meal. Not only is she a fine cook who writes gilded prose, but she is also a fellow sensualist – smitten as surely by the scent of wild weeds warm in the summer sun, as by the tensile yield of well-kneaded yeasted dough in the hands, captured as easily by the fragrance of a perfectly ripe peach as by the feel of soft rumpled, wheat-coloured linen.

Honestly, what were the chances? If the next day were not a bank holiday, my partner and I would not have traveled over to the Left Bank that evening for the artisanal olive oil. Had traffic not been utterly terrible, and had my foot not been severely bothering me after the morning's trek on a cookware quest to E. Dehillerin, we would not have stopped at Les Deux Magots to rest for a bit. And to meet an author I admire at a literary landmark – naturally Ms. de Blasi would want to sit at such a place – well, how *à-propos*.

"I don't want to bother her," I said, as I took another sip of my Provençal rosé and again glanced over at her seated at the front table.

"She'd love to hear how much you adore her books. I bet she'd be more thrilled than annoyed. Besides," my mate pointed out, "she's sitting at the very front table on the sidewalk... she's not exactly *hiding*."

I weighed the situation for ten minutes, swirling my salmon-hued wine in its glass and turning every so often to peer in her direction, all the while half-hearing the loud American couple to our right argue over the husband's limited cooking repertoire. I decided that I was not going to let the serendipitous moment slip away.

Her husband had briefly disappeared inside the restaurant, and I stood up, walked over to her table, and knelt down beside her.

"Excuse me, do you happen to be Marlena de Blasi?"

For just an instant, her wide eyes washed over with puzzlement, ebbing to surprise as she realized one of her fans had approached at a Paris café and was saying hello.

"Why, yes... I am... but... how did you know?"

"You look like your photos," I said, "I don't want to intrude or bother you, but I just have to tell you how much I adore your books."

She reached out and took my hands, looking deep into my eyes with something like astonishment. "I can't believe this," she said in a voice brimming with genuine amazement, "we've only just arrived an hour ago. And here you are, like an angel, saying hello to me. Please, tell me who you are... and how did you come to be here, just now?"

I told her how I adored her skill with language and stories, that I was a fellow chef, an author, that I had lived abroad for several years and had read all of her books... that I had read several of them aloud to my mate, even.

"But you haven't read them all," she interrupted and smiled as she grasped my hand, her palms wrapped in charcoal lace. "I have a new one that comes out on the 23rd. If you give me your address, I will send it to you!"

A few moments later, her husband Fernando, who features prominently in several of her books, reappeared, and introductions passed round the small table.

"He's a chef! He's a writer! He used to live abroad! He loves the books!" she exclaimed to Fernando in Italian. I kept trying to break away, not wanting to intrude further on their café experience, but she wouldn't let me go.

Ten minutes later, my mate had come to the table and been introduced as well. She said yes to taking a photo together. When I finally made an exit, leaving them at their front table and walking into the crowd with my partner, I was blessed by her wide-eyed, somewhat emotional benediction, "We are tribe."

In my hand on a piece of paper, I carried her personal email address – with instructions to write to her, and a promise to send me a copy of the forthcoming book.

For all the world, she (and Fernando) could not have been more gracious. Even as cliché as it sounds, I will always remember those first moments of meeting Marlena.

What a delight to be able to share from my heart – the heart of a cook, an artist, a lover of stories and well-spun words – how deeply I have savored her works. Honestly, encountering Ms. de Blasi at Les Deux Magots was something more than the star-gazing thrill of crossing paths with a celebrity. Rather it was the pleasure of meeting someone who walks through the world with senses cast wide and heart ajar, a fellow Soul Artist – one who finds delight in little details, who knows that beauty, pleasure, and simple, rustic food prepared with best quality ingredients, all feed the soul.

"Now *that* was destiny," exclaimed Robert as we walked away.

I'm inclined to agree. At the very least, it was enough to restore my faith in the inexplicable forces that guide the shifting currents of our lives towards unseen, mysterious ends.

Paris has always been special for me, a place of life-changing experiences. Now, when I am fortunate enough to return there in the future, when I stroll through St.-Germain-des-Prés, or pass Les Deux Magots – or even when I simply think of Paris – I will certainly recall the spring afternoon when a curious string of events conspired to bring me face to face with Marlena de Blasi.

And I can hardly wait for *The Umbrian Thursday Night Supper Club*.

❧ ❧ ❧

Singing the Pagan Moon: All Hallows' Eve

(October 2016; written 2010, England)

Al Hallows Eve. It feels as if the entire day has been lifted from a spooky, storybook tale with ghostly trees draped in mist and fog. Along our quiet, rural lane in West Sussex, there are no children ringing doorbells for "trick or treat," though I suspect that they are out in force in the village. Just as precaution, however, the gate is shut and the front light is off, so that from outside it seems no one is at home. The hermit has no wish for children calling at his door.

The moon is nearly full, suspended like a luminous pearl set amid folds of dark grey silk, and all the night is bathed in silvery light. Standing on the stone terrace in the chilly darkness and gazing up, I watch thin veils of clouds drawn quickly across the sky.

Since ancient times in Britain, 31 October has been celebrated as a gathering of the harvest and a feast for the dead. Known as Samhain ("SAW-win", "SAW-vane" or "SOW-ain") in neo-pagan circles, the Gaelic word means "summer's end". All Hallows Eve (*hallow* means "to sanctify") bore many names: Hallowtide; Hallowmass; Hallows; All Souls Night; Day of the Dead. It marked the start of the Celtic new year, and the beginning of the lean, cold months ahead, as the last of the crops were gathered and celebrated with festivals and fairs. Where possible, livestock were brought in from the fields and kept in sheds until spring; some were slaughtered, their meat preserved to offer sustenance through the long, dark winter. Beginning at sundown, it was a time of thanks and for honoring the dead, offering prayers and food left on altars and doorsteps, and generally one of only two nights of the year when the hearth fires were extinguished (Beltane being the other).

The ancient Celts, in particular, viewed Samhain as an auspicious time, a cross-quarter day situated halfway between the autumnal equinox and winter solstice. The spiritual veil between worlds was considered to be at its thinnest (along with Beltane six months opposite on the calendar wheel), when beings from the otherworld could emerge and be seen. With the spirit world so near at hand, the night offered an open window for magic and communion, and the dead were often invited to feast with their earthly kin left behind – a place set at the table and cakes set outside the door.

Whether I call it All Hallows Eve, Samhain, or Day Of The Dead, it seems an appropriate time to acknowledge my own ancestors and give thanks for the blessings in my life. It has long been my custom to recognize this night of portent with some kind of quiet ceremony, either with others or in solitude. Tonight, I will roam alone under the streaming pale clouds and offer my gratitude to the Universe, scattering intentions like seeds upon the rich, dark earth.

The air is not overly cold but I wrap the soft charcoal ribbon of cashmere just a bit more snugly around my neck, having decided to forego wearing my wool cap. Stepping forth from the cottage, walking across the front garden toward the deer fence and brightly shimmering fields beyond, I step through the tall gate and, for a moment, have the impression of crossing some threshold into a mysterious other realm beyond my familiar one. I cannot describe exactly what gives this feeling, but I note the slight tingling sensation in my body and a sense of being drawn just slightly more open, as if pulled by gossamer strands or perhaps tiny invisible hands.

The night world is flooded in silvery light, bright enough that my eyes hardly need to adjust. I certainly don't need a "torch" or flashlight. Even in the moonlight, I detect the hues of russet, copper and gold of the surrounding hillsides, faded and mute beneath the racing clouds. The footpath through the wet grass easily visible, along the edge of the recently planted field I walk, its broad expanse already sprouting up with slim green shoots of winter wheat.

I don't have a set route in my head, content instead to let my feet simply carry me where they may into the glimmering dark. A rustic, elk hide rattle protrudes from my back pocket, and I've a small candle and some blood red corn kernels tucked in my coat, the humble makings of an offering. Passing the great oak who stands sentinel at the edge of the fields, still crowned with gilded leaves but ever more naked as the days grow colder, his form aglow and majestic in the moonlight, I bow to him and veer right to follow the hedgerow down into the hollow.

As I descend the slope of the hill, the hedge ends at a copse of dark trees, a tangled spur that emerges from a larger wood on my left, while to my right, the field is a silver and green blanket draped across the gentle hill. Continuing along the footpath, I am traversing the cusp of two different realms: shadowy, whispering woods, and the bright, open, moonlit field. Darkness meets light. An *edgewalker*, I am.

Something unseen launches from the trees, startling me with the sudden noise of its flight. A wood pigeon, perhaps, or some other winged one disturbed by my passing. In the wooded darkness on my left, I hear the crashing of a moderate-sized animal moving rapidly through the thickets, darting away.

The tangled shadows teem with energy and sounds, while the field rests open and silent, and the autumnal perfume of wood smoke from a distant chimney wafts through the cool air.

Lost in the noises and scents of the misty darkness, I suddenly draw up short, halted by the sight of the trees just ahead where the edge of the field juts around another spur of the wood. In the silvery night, the bare trees are revealed as elegant spirits, rising up with naked arms like dancers, reaching for the pearl of moon. So humanlike in this expression are they, that I stop in my tracks, and for a shining moment I do not see them as trees at all; instead I perceive their true essence and inner nature. Gazing upwards, following the thousand fingers that extend heavenwards, I note that the sky is clear and the great silver jewel is encircled in a luminous moonbow.

This is the place, I decide.

Somewhere in the distance of the dark wood, the small, hooting voice of an owl calls out.

Yes, *definitely* the right place.

I pull the handmade percussive instrument from my back pocket and begin to shake it in a wide circle about my body, hearing the small stones inside wake to life, singing with their familiar voices as I rattle loudly toward the dancing trees and brightly glowing moon.

For an instant, the familiar censor whispers in my brain, *what if someone is out walking and hears or sees you?*

Who cares, I shrug, shaking the rattle more loudly. I'm just a crazy man on the edge of a field and wood on a night of ancient magic, dancing at the threshold of light and shadow. In my low voice, still hoarse from my recent chest infection, I call out to silver shadows. I acknowledge Earth, trees, the field, the grasses and soil, furry moles underfoot and microbes whirling everywhere, the unseen earthly creatures, the spirits of field and wood and earth and air. I hail my own ancestors and departed family, Gaia and the Moon as embodiments of the Divine Feminine, and the Sacred Masculine.

It's a decidedly eclectic roll call, embracing both the mystic and material, the living and dead. Humbly, I acknowledge my small place in the much larger relationship that enfolds, speaking aloud to the interconnectedness of everything.

Still waving my trusty rattle with its rhythmic chorus of pebbly voices, I offer a song to the radiant, haloed moon.

Here in the fold between field and wood, the air is still, as if the night itself is listening. Crouching down, I pull the slim candle from my pocket, light its wick using a purple plastic lighter, and push the flickering taper into soft, yielding soil. A phallic, masculine flame rising up from the receptive earth.

Speaking aloud, I offer my gratitude to the night, giving thanks for uncountable blessings in my life. One by one, I speak to my dead family and unknown ancestors, acknowledging and thanking them for the gifts passed down to me.

Removing the corn kernels from my coat pocket, I toss the ruby gems one by one into the tall grass, each a garnet prayer. These blood red seeds, carried from New Mexico, are a symbolic offering of thanks as I speak to the night. The purpose is decidedly not planting New World corn alongside an English wood, but to symbolically cast my intentions within the Unified Field. I suspect that the grains will most likely end up in a pheasant's gullet, and I'm happy to share what I can with the 'more-than-human' world around me. Let others be nourished by what I've scattered.

May we all be fed.

When my unrehearsed chant of gratitude and prayer feels complete, I crouch down to retrieve the flickering candle, a dodgy knee groaning in the process. Blowing out the flame, I shake the drops of wax to the earth and place the small taper again into my coat. Rattle finds its way to my back pocket.

In the shadowy fields of Sussex, another Samhain rolls into mist and memory. The naked trees continue to dance and sing to the heavens as I move on, ascending along the edge of the field towards the crest of the hill. Looking out across the shimmering night, cream has poured into the hollows and low places, making dark islands of trees and hilltops as the fog swirls around.

What a gift to be alive and savoring this moment of beauty beneath a magic moon, giving thanks for uncountable blessings and mysterious grace.

Silently, I begin walking back towards the cottage, treading on a dark serpent of path through the wet grass. I've not worn my Wellingtons or waterproof boots and before long my shoes and socks are soaked through. Cold. In the distance, just where I expect it to be, the cheery yellow glow of our cottage lights emerge in the darkness, a warm and homey beacon.

Stepping back through the high deer gate left ajar, again I sense that I've crossed over some invisible, psychic boundary, now returning to the familiar realms instead of magical ones. Outside the front door of the little brick house with its steeply gabled roof, though I'm eager to remove wet boots and warm my chilled feet, I gaze up for a final look at the silver coin in the sky, noting that clouds completely veil its face, just as when I first set out.

How is it that only in the hollow of the dancing trees, on the cusp between darkness and light, that She appeared in a clear sky, surrounded by a moonbow? On this magic night, it was as if the veil between worlds drew back and I stepped through to a place of hushed power and trembling beauty. I smile, privy to some numinous secret, and then open the door to the welcoming light and warmth of the cottage.

A fine night indeed for crossing between realms, honoring the ancestors, giving thanks, and singing to a pagan moon.

Blessed be.

🍂 🍂 🍂

A Return to Center: Welcoming the Healer
(May 2016)

N estled among the magical redwoods, in the hushed stillness of a Mendocino farmhouse, serenaded by a chorus of frogs in the green pond that my room overlooked, I slept and dreamed.

A deep, healing sleep it was, not waking once for eleven hours, cocooned in a sense of being stitched back together at a cellular level, some sort of essential transformation going on, seemingly down to my DNA itself. When I finally woke in the soft morning light, it was like emerging from a long journey and discovering that I had finally come home to myself.

Last weekend, I went away north to the tall trees for a weekend of insight and healing—a secret ayahuasca ceremony—to reflect upon my path in the world and what I offer. In the end, what I realized is that the heart of my work, which I have long identified as being centered upon *nourishment,* is really about *healing.* This might seem obvious to some who know me, but oddly it wasn't that clear to myself.

Ever since my days at the Boulder College of Massage Therapy some twenty-five years ago, I have been leery of the word "healer." It always carried a slightly sticky, somewhat self-important note to it, and too often worn as a badge for the ego. When people said of themselves, "I'm a healer," some part of me simply wanted to roll my eyes, for I've long understood that healing comes from somewhere beyond, and it is not something any of us can take credit for. In hands-on sessions and coaching, I have witnessed clients undergo remarkable transformations, but it was never *me* that healed them; it is some other grace for which I was simply a conduit.

Too many people call themselves healers who haven't done their own work. They don't live a healer's lifestyle, and some of them are profoundly unhealthy. Whether with television, junk food, or any other modern addiction, they fill their bodies, minds, and energetic fields with garbage. It's true that some of them do possess genuine gifts, but identifying as a "healer" bolsters an otherwise low self-esteem or self-importance, and makes them feel good about themselves. I challenge you: if your own life isn't about the highest transformation and evolution possible, how can you possibly be a *healer?*

And so I've always steered clear of the term and title, choosing instead to simply focus upon offering nourishment for body and soul as my path, both public and private, whether that role was bodyworker, coach/guide, chef, or as a writer. Indeed, it is one of the central, recurring themes in this weekly column: *what nourishes the bodysoul?*

These past months have been a time of powerful transformation for me, triggered partly by my electromagnetic hypersensitivity (EHS) forcing me to lay aside my work with others despite the financial anxiety and squeeze of that (which offered its own healing and lessons), while venturing farther into realms of healing and earth connection. It has been an Underworld journey of sorts; a passage into shadows and vulnerability, and emerging on the other side, transformed and carrying a gift.

This past weekend's retreat to the redwoods marked the culmination of that journey – at least to the extent that I am able to perceive it now – and brought me back to center; embracing my deeper work, understanding that is what my soul came back here to do in this lifetime. More than that, it means finally picking up the term and placing it across my chest: *healer.*

"A healer who writes," is what I just yesterday updated my website biography to read.

It isn't self-important, congratulatory, or a crutch for my ego, but simply the truth. Everything about my life is centered upon healing: from the rituals of a deliberately built existence free of television and media, to the fresh, organic food that I prepare with gratitude and share with others, giving up everything that doesn't support that higher work or my highest well-being (including sugar, caffeine, wheat, meat, and alcohol), and embracing a deep connection with nature and the soul of the world.

I will continue to write books but it feels like an important shift, this letting go of identifying as an *author* (and all the baggage that goes with that) and coming home to the heart of healing.

In our own ways, each of us is looking for healing. We might call that a quest for *meaning*, or *wholeness*, or *connection*; it might be a spiritual path or searching for our place in the world. Yet all of these are simply other facets of *healing* and the process of finding our own light, along with the gift we have to offer.

Dozens of times in this journal I have written that Soul Artists are radically authentic people who continually seek to offer something of beauty and value to the world. Truly, the soul's journey and the healing path are the same (or so closely entwined as to be nearly indistinguishable): emerging past what limits and restrains us, opening the heart wider, practicing forgiveness, and diving headlong into the darkest depths of ourselves.

As I sat in the old wooden chair near the pond's edge, writing in my little journal with my trusty old fountain pen while listening to a raven laughing gutturally from a high redwood perch, I realized that much of healing is about the spirit of *empowerment*. It is the receipt and assumption of power, igniting a vital life energy within us, that bestows a tenacity and determination to succeed in becoming our most authentic, creative, and unlimited self. Exactly like soul work.

Friend, what is it in your life that needs healing? And what are you willing to give up or sacrifice in order to embrace that transformation? We are all learning how to transform and let go of our past. Remember that your very words have power, including the ways that you speak of and identify yourself and your being in the world.

Here's hoping you'll move toward healing as you face your inner and outer work, letting go of the past that keeps you tethered, coming home to a true sense of yourself. And may you embrace forgiveness, soul courage and grace in all that you do.

Blessed be.

❧ ❧ ❧

Kneel and Kiss the Earth: One Man's Prayer

(November 2015)

The sea is rumbling and agitated. Even a half mile away in a quiet neighborhood dense with evergreen trees, I hear its low voice, timeless and primordial. Louder than normal.

I have been feeling restless myself, and burdened by carrying a basket of grumbles that I wish I could lay aside. What I need is to sit beneath the arms of a noble, gnarled oak and plant each disappointment as if it were a darkly burnished acorn, recognizing the secret gift of it, and count my blessings instead. Or toss each heavy stone, glinting as it flies, into the ocean's fathomless depths.

The poet Rumi wrote, *There are a thousand ways to kneel and kiss the ground; there are a thousand ways to go home again.*

Whenever I am out of sorts – blue, restless, unwell, disappointed – I need to touch the earth, feel it soft and yielding beneath my footsteps. Always, this is the embrace that I must return to. *Tell me what you love*, a voice breathes in a whisper as the wind rustles the surrounding trees, *and I will remind you who you are.*

Here, now. Kiss the ground. Open your heart to everything and touch the sacred in this moment, whispering, *holy... holy.*

In the chilled, hushed air of sunrise, softly I speak aloud, as if sharing a secret between us. Each word a prayer, a wisp of blue fragrant smoke, calling my soul home to itself while simultaneously invoking and praising something much larger.

Earth under my feet, I am reminded that I spend too much time in my head rather than dancing, roaming the trails of coastal canyons, or sitting quietly on a hillside and listening to forgotten voices – the ones who would tell me everything if only I would listen; the ones who remind me that I am not my thoughts, but something much more embodied and real.

As flesh, bone, and breath, it's such a short time we inhabit this beautiful earth – each of us a unique constellation of creativity and warmly animated matter that will never again be duplicated in exactly the same way. My time here is more valuable than merely *work* with its notions of progress, success, or merit.

The modern world we inhabit is mostly an illusion; a paper economy made of electronic phantoms, numbers on a computer screen. We base our worth on a collective societal agreement that the pieces of cloth-paper we carry in our wallets have value, and that such value varies according to whatever numbers or faces are printed upon them. We have traded gold coins for slips of parchment, our souls for corporate jobs, and wildness for domesticity.

The sacred has been banished, hand in hand with mystery.

Here, now, with dried cypress needles underfoot and the rumbling voice of the sea, this is what's real – not my number of Facebook "friends" or Twitter followers, not my accomplishments or seeming failures, nor the evening news. I don't want more information, that's simply smoke and mirrors – mental masturbation for my brain. No, no, no. Fill my heart, instead.

Give me birdsong, amber bees loving the fragrant lavender flowers, and a luminous sunset that feeds my hungry soul. Shatter me with heart-stopping beauty that makes me reach for my beloved's hand, squeezing it tightly. I want unrestrained, embodied sex that shakes my entire body, crashing wildly with waves of sensation and making me howl at the moon. May I be filled with sunny thoughts that drift leisurely like clouds of changing shape, not a list of things to do by three o'clock, or a punctuated stream of superficial comments online.

Bare feet on the ground, morning breeze touching my face, I am listening. We are surrounded by stories, each thing in humming relationship with everything else, but we have forgotten – or never learned – how to listen. We do not hear the summoning, voiceless words that enquire:

Who are you, and what do you bring?

What do you know of your wild soul?

How do you stand in relationship to the many realms of interconnected reality?

What will you offer of yourself without shame or apology? And what will you leave behind for the benefit of others ... for Earth?

Draped in pastel hues of dawn and dusk, these are the questions – the only ones worth living in this short span of existence.

Yet, too often I forget both the queries and answers I have found. Or I doubt that what I bring is worthy and has value. *Real* value, like sweet, golden carrots dug from dark soil and piled in the kitchen sink, or a supper lovingly made from fresh garden bounty and placed upon the table amid flickering beeswax candles. Or the wrinkles at the edge of my beloved's eyes when we laugh at the absurdity of it all, the moments we look back fondly upon as life slips quietly away, one day at a time. *That* kind of value.

I ask myself, *why do you worry so?* Why cannot I trust that I am guided, protected, and cared for in each moment, that everything that happens is simply an opportunity for growth, no matter how difficult it seems? Why do I slip back into the illusion, seeing myself as separate and my actions mechanical, when I know all is connected and in conscious relationship with everything else?

Grace abounds, often manifesting in the most curious, unexpected manner. And when we offer something from the soul, the Universe responds in kind.

This moment, flowing seamlessly into the next in a lifestream of spirit, will never come again. The challenge is to wake up from the modern dream world and technological trance, to step outside the four walls that contain us. Life isn't about slips of cloth-paper in your wallet or figures on a printout from the bank, nor the number of readers of an article, books sold or not. Rather, it's the grass under your feet, your wildly beating heart, rolling tides of breath, and the hum inside your cells.

Here, now. Listen to the wind as it rustles the trees, giving them an audible voice. Catch the comments of the twittering birds, the distant chant of the ocean. Inhale the resinous fragrance of cypress and evergreens, the faint tangy note of the coastal air. Breathe in, breathe out. Remember who you are.

Move your tired bones, let your body bend and sway. Descend from your head into your heart. Let Earth be the thing that you love, knowing that it sustains us and that we are inseparable from it. Can you love her as deeply and passionately as the beloved still sleeping in your bed? Or your children and family, human or four-legged? The earth is no less deserving of your tender gaze, gentle touch, your velvet-soft words of praise and appreciation.

At moments, I forget what I know in my heart. And I take life too damn seriously.

So I step outside my small cottage, listening to the churning sea in the distance, my unclad soles meeting the cool ground and, if only for a while, I set my basket of mental burdens on the porch. On the horizon, a bright star of morning glimmers like a diamond. *Look up, this way, and follow me.* Once more I am inspired to take up my dreams, wrapped in the tattered silk of prayers, and go on, one foot after the other, heading west into mystery and climbing the mountain.

The world desperately needs a compassionate man's heart, and I offer mine forward, beating and strong. Weeping, sometimes, for the ache and losses of life, great and small. Let me live my days as a wild love prayer to the Beloved.

How do we rewild the heart? Tear off the bandages. Turn off the computer and your phone. Go outdoors and breathe the unconditioned air. Lay your hands upon the roughly furrowed bark of a venerable tree and gaze up at the sky through its tangled branches, shifting your perspective. Shed your shoes. Feel the earth under your bare feet, connecting with what's real. Come back to life. With each breath, return home to yourself.

Then kneel and kiss the ground, covered with painted leaves.

Holy, holy.

❧ ❧ ❧

Acknowledgments

During the years of writing the *Soul Artist Journal*, from many sources I constantly drew inspiration, perspective, strength, and the willingness to continue with my weekly *giveaway*. A few of those dear souls and resources deserve special mention.

☙

Gaia, the Wild Beloved. We tend to use the word "nature" as if it were something *out there*, separate from ourselves, when in fact, right down to our microbes, we are indivisible and inseparable from the *suprasomatic sentience* in which we are constantly steeped. Yet I remain deeply indebted to the wild shorelines, verdant fields, whispering woods, and dry arroyos where I have walked, seeking solace and inspiration. Healing. And magic. Endless blessings to the noble trees.

All the readers of the Journal. As stated in the Preface, it was you that so often kept me going—especially when I felt reluctant (unable, even) to deliver another Sunday offering. Bless you for reading, sharing, and the lovely comments via email and Facebook. It was my great privilege to offer you these glimpses of beauty, magic, wonder, and mysterious grace as nourishment for the soul.

Sara, the Good Witch of Kent. Steadfast reader, confidant, and super-spooky friend. I surely would not have made it through all the shadows and pitfalls without your friendship, emails, and generous parcels of goodies. I've said it before: you remain the very best that England has to offer. Please do come round for tea tomorrow, darling.

Robert, *mon petit*. Really, there are no adequate words, love. Bless you for everything, every day. I go on choosing you, and we go onwards together, searching for home but always creating it in our hearts, wherever the painted gypsy caravan may be parked; a couple of flickering candles on the table, something delicious on our plates, and two lazy English Whippets underfoot. *Je t'aime... toujours.*

❧ ❧ ❧

About the Author

L.R. Heartsong is a healer who writes, teaching a sensual connection with life, nature, and the soul of the world.

A body-centered therapist trained in somatic psychology, he became a Paris-trained chef (briefly a cook for the rich and famous), until his intuition and heart led him back to the healing arts, along with nature-based soul work.

Living in England, a revelation while crossing a Kentish field at twilight propelled him to write *The Bones & Breath: A Man's Guide to Eros, the Sacred Masculine, and the Wild Soul.* Upon returning to America, as part of his quest to get the book published, he launched the *Soul Artist Journal,* which slowly grew in popularity.

After nearly five years of weekly posts (2012–2017), River closed the cover on the Journal and began *TendingSacred*—lengthier, monthly writing along a healer's path (2017–2019). He has been a featured presenter on multiple podcasts as well as global online symposiums featuring change-making influencers (scientists, shamans, mystics, psychologists, healers, and more).

His first book won a Nautilus Book Award for Personal Growth & Self-Help.

LRHeartsong.com